A FIELD BOOK FOR HIGHER EDUCATION LEADERS

A FIELD BOOK FOR HIGHER EDUCATION LEADERS

IMPROVING YOUR LEADERSHIP INTELLIGENCE

*Wanda Maulding Green
and Edward E. Leonard*

ROWMAN & LITTLEFIELD
Lanham • Boulder • New York • London

Published by Rowman & Littlefield
A wholly owned subsidiary of The Rowman & Littlefield Publishing Group, Inc.
4501 Forbes Boulevard, Suite 200, Lanham, Maryland 20706
www.rowman.com

Unit A, Whitacre Mews, 26-34 Stannary Street, London SE11 4AB

Copyright © 2018 by Wanda Maulding Green and Edward E. Leonard

All rights reserved. No part of this book may be reproduced in any form or by any electronic or mechanical means, including information storage and retrieval systems, without written permission from the publisher, except by a reviewer who may quote passages in a review.

British Library Cataloguing in Publication Information Available

Library of Congress Cataloging-in-Publication Data Available
ISBN: 978-1-4758-3902-9 (cloth : alk. paper)
ISBN: 978-1-4758-3903-6 (pbk. : alk. paper)
ISBN: 978-1-4758-3904-3 (electronic)

∞™ The paper used in this publication meets the minimum requirements of American National Standard for Information Sciences—Permanence of Paper for Printed Library Materials, ANSI/NISO Z39.48-1992.

Printed in the United States of America

CONTENTS

PREFACE	ix
ACKNOWLEDGMENTS	xi
INTRODUCTION	xiii
SITUATIONAL JUDGMENT TESTS	xix
1 LESSONS ON CREDIBILITY	1
Medically Incompetent	3
Small Things Matter	4
Exception to the Rule	5
A Helping Hand	6
Failure to Launch	7
A Bond Is Formed	8
2 AUTHORS' OPTIONS FOR CREDIBILITY-BASED SJTs	9
3 LESSONS ON COMPETENCE	13
How Much Is Enough?	15
Leadership Orientation	16
You're Not the Boss of Me	18
See and Be Seen	19
Yelling	20
If It *Is* Broken, Fix It	21
Erasing 100 "Atta-Boys"	22

CONTENTS

4 AUTHORS' OPTIONS FOR COMPETENCE-BASED SJTs — 23

5 LESSONS ON THE ABILITY TO INSPIRE — 27
   Get Rid of the Leadership Class — 29
   Fraternity Days — 30
   Not My Job — 31
   A Rose By Any Other Name — 32
   Define "Nasty" — 33
   Publish or Perish — 34

6 AUTHORS' OPTIONS FOR ABILITY TO INSPIRE SJTs — 35

7 LESSONS ON VISION — 39
   A Vision — 41
   Little White Lies — 42
   A Bumpy Road to Success — 43
   Demanding to Defend — 44
   Spring Is in the Air — 46
   On The Road Again — 47

8 AUTHORS' OPTIONS FOR VISION SJTs — 49

9 LESSONS ON EMOTIONAL INTELLIGENCE/SOFT SKILLS — 53
   Compassion — 56
   A Stitch in Time — 57
   Fun at Work? — 58
   Ma'am, Would You Step Out of the Car, Please? — 60
   Self-Knowledge — 61
   Feet of Clay — 63
   Roommate Issues — 64
   Disappointment — 66

10 AUTHORS' OPTIONS FOR EMOTIONAL INTELLIGENCE/SOFT SKILLS SJTs — 67

   AUTHORS' SOLUTIONS FOR SJTs — 71
   CREDIBILITY SOLUTIONS — 73
   COMPETENCE SOLUTIONS — 77
   ABILITY TO INSPIRE SOLUTIONS — 81
   VISION SOLUTIONS — 85
   EMOTIONAL INTELLIGENCE/SOFT SKILLS SOLUTIONS — 89

CONTENTS

APPENDIX A: SMALL GROUP CARDS — 95

APPENDIX B: LSI INTERPRETATION CHART — 97

APPENDIX C: ACTIVITIES TO IMPROVE YOUR LEADERSHIP INTELLIGENCE — 99

NOTES — 103

ABOUT THE AUTHORS — 107

PREFACE

One of the key points in *Leadership Intelligence: Navigating to Your True North* is that the soft skills that comprise the major leadership intelligence areas of credibility, competence, inspirational ability, vision, and emotional intelligence can be learned. Leaders, aspiring leaders, or anyone who wishes to build their leadership capacity, with proper exposure and practice, can learn new skills or enhance skills they already possess. Learning or enhancing skills builds a leader's adaptive capacity. In *Geeks and Geezers: How Era, Values, and Defining Moments Shape Leaders*, Warren Bennis and Robert Thomas share that,

> To the extent that any single quality determines success, that quality is adaptive capacity. ... When we look at who becomes a leader, we see enormous variance in IQ, birth order, family wealth, family stability, level of education, ethnicity, race, and gender. Certainly, these factors cannot be dismissed entirely. But in studying both very young and older leaders, we found over and over again that much more important than a person's measured intelligence—to take just one factor—was his or her ability to transcend the limits that a particular IQ might impose. In the case of intelligence, this includes avoiding the trap of seeing oneself as highly intelligent, hopelessly average, or below average to the exclusion of other, more useful self-definitions. We emphatically agree with Ford's Elizabeth Kao that "everyone has their own wall to climb." And we believe that both the willingness to climb those walls and the ability to find ways to do so are the real measure of a leader.[1]

Bennis and Thomas go on to say that leaders "learn important lessons, including new skills that allow them to move on to new levels of achievement and new levels of learning. This ongoing process of challenge, adaptation, and learning prepares the individual for the next crucible, where the process is repeated. Whenever significant new problems are encountered and dealt with adaptively, new levels of competence are achieved, better preparing the individual for the next challenge."[2]

Summarizing the concept of adaptive capacity in later writing, Bennis reemphasizes the importance of adaptive capacity, saying, "the ruling quality of leaders, adaptive capacity, is what allows true leaders to make the nimble decisions that bring success."[3] Making correct decisions is based on three premises: knowledge of a given situation, technical "hard/competence based" skills, and "soft" people skills.

Knowledge of events will vary from situation to situation but leaders cannot succeed without the people skills that allow them to fully utilize their technical skills. It is the recognition of the importance of acquiring the requisite technical and people skills, and moving to acquire and/or enhance those skills as new discoveries or innovations occur or when new strategies develop, that is the cornerstone of building leadership intelligence that allows leader adaptive capacity to flourish.

A Field Book for Higher Education Leaders: Improving Your Leadership Intelligence takes the reader through a series of situational judgment tests (SJTs) that address the soft skill areas that lead to success. The SJTs are drawn from real-life experiences and are testament to the challenges, large and small, that a leader faces and the leadership intelligence and adaptive capacity a leader must exercise to make correct decisions. Developing or enhancing your leadership intelligence and adaptive capacity, and thereby your ability to make proper decisions, is a foundational leadership ability.

This book takes you on a leadership development journey into the real-life world of leadership in higher education. It is a leadership world directed at educating each student. As Catherine Bond Hill, president of Vassar College, shared in her 2010 address to the Vassar spring convocation:

> What could better capture the ideal of the education that we've aspired to provide? It is an education that is less about defining a path, rather very much an education that allows one to choose paths—the open road. It is an education that creates options—lifelong options—through both having nurtured a robust curiosity and having developed the tools necessary to satisfy that curiosity. So you have options . . . leading wherever you choose, the world before you.[4]

ACKNOWLEDGMENTS

Once more we would like thank Tom Koerner for his enthusiastic support of this field book. We are truly grateful for the opportunities Tom has afforded us and hope he is pleased with the results. We would also like to thank the R & L team who always work so diligently behind the scenes from inception through production.

And again, both Ed and I are truly grateful for amazing spouses. To Mrs. L (Carolyn Leonard), Ed sends a special thank you. Thank you for your support from reading and editing to encouragement and enthusiasm. And thank you, Steve Green, for your wisdom and insights and incredible cheerleading. You both have been instrumental in the completion of all of the *Leadership Intelligence* works in print and those yet to come.

INTRODUCTION

THE CONCEPT OF LEADERSHIP INTELLIGENCE

Leadership intelligence (LSI) is defined as "a construct that represents the level of leadership capacity an individual possesses at any given time. It addresses the characteristics, dispositions, and the 'soft' people/relational skills of individuals including: credibility, competence, ability to inspire, vision, and emotional intelligence."[1] Each of these major areas is subdivided into knowledge, skills, and dispositions as shown in the table on the next page. Each of the subscale items lend themselves to defining the major category.

Accompanying *Leadership Intelligence: Navigating to Your True North* is the leadership intelligence (LSI) assessment. It includes the subscale items listed in the foregoing table that the LSI assessment is designed to measure. Ideally, the best starting point for using this handbook is to take the LSI assessment, if you have not yet done so. The assessment is available free of charge online at http://www.leadershipintelligencelsi.com/copy-of-your-lsi-score.

This is a self-assessment and it is vitally important that you are absolutely candid in your responses. The results of the assessment will give you a snapshot of your leadership capacity. It is important for the test taker to acknowledge, however, that the assessment is a fluid one. You may take it today after a great day at work and reveal a higher score than you might, for instance, if you take it when you have had many difficult days as a leader.

For a broader look at your leadership capacity, the authors suggest that you conduct a 360-evaluation (alternately referred to as a circle assessment) by having people you work with, those who evaluate you, or those who work *for* you complete the survey.

INTRODUCTION

The Five Leader Imperatives of the Leadership GPS Model

CREDIBILITY	COMPETENCE	INSPIRATION	VISION	EMOTIONAL INTELLIGENCE
In 500 feet, stay right	**Recalculating**	**Satellite reception lost**	**You have arrived at your destination**	**Route guidance suggested**
Ethics or Personal Accountability	Discernibility	Enthusiastic	Commitment	Resilience
Honesty	Perception	Energetic	Sense of Direction	Communication and Listening
Responsibility	Conflict Resolution Skills	Passionate	Professionalism	Happiness
Trust	Problem-Solving and Decision-Making Skills	Optimistic	Decisive	Personality Traits
Integrity	Relationship Building	Genuine	Work Ethic	Sense of Humor
Sincerity	Planning and Implementation	Courageous	Concern for the Future	Assertiveness
	Assessment and Evaluation			Flexibility
				Empathy/ Interpersonal Interactions

Source: Wanda S. Maulding Green and Edward E. Leonard, *Leadership Intelligence: Navigating to Your True North* (Lanham, MD: Rowman & Littlefield, 2016), p. 19.

Conducting a 360-assessment to accompany your self-assessment will provide you with a measure of the match or congruence of your view of your leadership capacity with the view of others directly associated with you as a leader or aspiring leader. You may do this by inquiring on the website via the "Contact Us" page at http://www.leadershipintelligencelsi.com/. Based on the results of your self-assessment and/or your 360-assessment, you are ready to work through *A Field Book for Higher Education Leaders: Improving Your Leadership Intelligence*.

However, taking the assessment is not required to make good use of the field book. The scenarios provided are a source from which to develop insight into and familiarity with the kinds of real-life situations with which higher education leaders or leaders in general must deal. Most of the events described in the field manual are encountered by any leader (perhaps in slightly different contexts). Leaders share many commonalities in terms of the issues they must address, especially soft skill, people-related issues.

INTRODUCTION

HOW TO USE THE FIELD BOOK INDIVIDUALLY

Use of the field book is straightforward and simple. There are thirty-three scenarios based on the five constructs of LSI (leadership intelligence). All of the scenarios are higher education–based but are potentially adaptive to all leadership situations.

Select a scenario. Read the scenario carefully. Think about the situation described and the possible solutions. Jot down in the space provided the solution you think would lead to the best outcome for the scenario. Then jot down a rationale for your solution.

After you have completed this part of the activity, turn to the section where the "Authors' Options" are located. Read the options carefully and choose a best response from those listed. (Note: Each scenario lists a final option that is blank. If you believe your solution is better than those provided by the authors, you should pencil it in.)

With your solution and rationale in hand and your choice from the "Authors' Options" list (or your own solution), turn to the section of the field book titled "Authors' Solutions for SJTs" to see the authors' solution* to the SJT (listed by chapter and scenario). Compare your own solution and rationale to the authors' solutions. Close alignment of your solution and rationale with that of the solutions provided suggests a well-honed sense of analysis of the situation. It is important to realize, though, that while some solutions and the accompanying rationale are better than others, there is often more than one acceptable way to resolve an issue or situation.

As a last step to gain further insight, the authors encourage you to peruse the complementary suggested reading cited from *Leadership Intelligence: Navigating to Your True North* as well as the additional selected reading listed at the end of each scenario. Follow this same cycle as you read and work through the field manual.

*Disclaimer: At the end of the book are the authors' recommended solutions, rationale, and reasoning for rejection of alternative solutions. These recommendations are in no way intended to supersede work policy or act as legal advice to the learner. If you encounter similar situations, you should consult with the proper authorities and/or act as you deem appropriate based on your own judgment. The situational judgment test (SJT) scenarios included are based on actual situations encountered by the authors, including the solutions they enacted at the time and place of the circumstance, and these may or may not be appropriate today individually or in your place of work.

HOW TO USE THE FIELD BOOK WITH GROUPS OR INSTRUCTIONALLY

Using the field book as an instructional tool follows the same general pattern as for individual use with some differences. Divide the class into small groups. Provide each group with an SJT scenario. Instruct the group members to read the scenario carefully, think about the situation described and the possible solutions, and jot down individually in the space provided how they would respond to the scenario. Then jot down a rationale for the solution.

After each individual has completed this part of the activity, the facilitator should direct the groups to the "Authors' Options" section. Individually, again, the class members should choose a best response from those listed. (Note: Each scenario lists a final option that is blank. If students believe their solution is better than those provided by the authors, they should pencil it in.)

Next, time should be allowed within the small groups for individuals to share their choices and come to a group consensus on the best solution. Time should also be allowed for discussion and dialogue regarding the rationale for the individual choices. (Prior to class, instructors should prepare answer-sharing cards to be utilized for this part of the activity. See appendix A for an example.) After ample small group discussion time has been given, the instructor should ask the small groups to *raise the card* with the letter of the solution they have chosen.

The instructor should then guide the large group instruction regarding the choices the small groups have made with ensuing dialogue. All of this rich discourse is intended to help *grow* the participants' "adaptive capacity" for leadership. Additionally, the instructor may choose to share the "Authors' Solutions" rationale, along with the rationale for rejection of the other choices. Repeat the process for each SJT scenario.

Whether used individually or in a group setting, the use of SJTs adds an element of realism to the concepts presented. Situational judgment tests (SJTs) also allow readers to utilize their analytical skills and judgment in synthesizing a solution and rationale. Each of these are required in a leadership situation as any decision can and, in all likelihood, will be examined and criticized, and a leader must be able to defend his or her decisions.

Finally, to fully solidify the learning from the class, the complementary reading from *Leadership Intelligence: Navigating to Your True North* is listed at the end. Additionally, relevant, contemporary selected related readings are presented at the end of each scenario to solidify the learning gained through practice.

HEADED IN THE RIGHT DIRECTION?

The conceptual model for leadership intelligence is a GPS system. With that framework in mind, there are many "directions" you might take to get to a final destination. As such, you may review your leadership intelligence assessment (LSI) and determine to work on the area where your score was lowest. That is fine. For example, you might skip over to the chapter with scenarios pertaining to "vision," if that works best for you. The field book was designed to be used individually, if desired.

If you are an instructor working with a class, the quickest route to your destination might be to work through from the beginning to the end. On the other hand, you might

INTRODUCTION

want to vary the scenarios to accommodate everyone in your class rather than going through each topic before moving to the next. For you, getting to your destination might include waypoints along the route.

For all, the main thing to remember is that there are many ways to get to a specific destination. There is more than one correct way to solve a problem, and the quickest route to a solution may not always be the wisest. As you work through the scenarios, you will gain confidence in your navigational skills and become a better leader along the way.

SITUATIONAL JUDGMENT TESTS

Situational judgment tests (SJTs) are assessments where the test taker is presented with a real or hypothetical situation and is then asked to select the most appropriate response to that scenario. SJTs have been around since the early 1920s. They have been used for garnering feedback from leaders in a variety of situations, from those in managerial positions in the workplace to those responsible for decision making in the military.[1] Over the years, SJTs have proved to be good predictors of job performance. The authors believe they are a good tool to use, especially for a field book such as this one because, as McDaniel and coauthors put it, SJTs:

- have low adverse impact
- assess soft skills
- have good acceptance by applicants
- assess job-related skills not tapped by other measures, and
- assess "nonacademic," practical intelligence.[2]

With those considerations in mind, the situational judgment test is an excellent tool to use when growing one's skill set in leadership intelligence. As stated above, the typical format of a situational judgment test is for a brief scenario to be shared with the learner. Of course, this sharing may be done via video clip, live role-play, or in a written form. After the student acknowledges the situation, typically, they are given multiple-choice responses to review and select from. In this field book, an additional step is added.

Prior to exposure to the author's multiple-choice answer options, the student is allowed to pen their own brief response to the scenario. This is done to allow the opportunity for rapid processing of *typical* thought processes: "What would I do in this situation without suggestion from others?" It allows the reader to reflect on his or her own "gut-level" response before being guided. This step, the internalization of an individual's usual or typical response, is critical in the growth aspect of this learning process.

It is important, then, for the reader to respond in the space provided as quickly and as honestly as possible. The reader should not be asking, "how *should* I respond?" but rather, "how have I responded to a similar problem in the past?" or even "what do I think is the best way to respond?"

For the classroom teacher, instructor, or workshop facilitator, situational judgment tests have the best outcomes when the situation is presented to an individual (or group of individuals) via "live" mechanisms, that is, role-play, video cast, or podcast. However, they are still effective when shared only in written form.

Traditionally, SJTs come in a variety of formats and responding mechanisms. Some require the participants to rank-order the stated options; others ask the participants to give only the *best* answer; still others call for the *unacceptable* responses. For the most part, the SJTs included in this field book ask for the participant to give the best response.

Additionally, the authors have (at the end of the book) given the "Authors' Solutions" to the SJTs (whether correct or incorrect); these are intended as best responses with rationales for the decisions and, similarly, the authors have provided their rationales for accepting or rejecting the other choice options. The most important takeaway for these exercises is to help the reader hear a range of potential responses to a situation and for the participants, over time, to become reflective learners.

The richness of these assessments comes via the facilitation of an invested leader, through individual, small group, and large group sharing and interaction. It is through these mechanisms that the best and most rapid learning can take place. Suggested readings from the companion book, *Leadership Intelligence: Navigating to Your True North*, follow each scenario but should not preempt the SJT itself. Selected additional readings that are relevant and contemporary are also presented at the end of each scenario to solidify the learning gained through practice.

Situational judgment tests were selected as the primary tool to help students grow their own leadership intelligence. These learnings, as shared in *Leadership Intelligence: Navigating to Your True North*, take time and repetitive activity to establish as norms as they are acquired in the most basal or primary parts of our brains.

1

LESSONS ON CREDIBILITY

One of the things that people notice about a leader, possibly more than any other thing a leader does, is the extent to which their actions are consistent with their articulated positions. Followers are asking and answering (to their own satisfaction) a vital question about each of their leaders. Do they say what they mean and support that with their actions? The answer to that question defines the credibility of the leader.

The scenarios in this chapter are, in one way or another, related to a leader's credibility. If your LSI assessment scores indicate this as an area for needed growth, you should work through the scenarios with a couple of things in mind. First, take particular note of the "Authors' Options" section, which provides responses to each problem at the end of each chapter of SJTs.

In working through the scenarios and reviewing the "Authors' Options," one of two things will happen. You will find disparity between your responses and those of the authors, or you might, indeed, find that your responses coincide with the authors' (see appendix B for a graphic representation). Next, reflect on the information you gained from the LSI assessment. If you acknowledge that credibility is an area for growth based on the assessment, ask yourself if this was based on your self-assessment, the circle assessment, or both.

If either or both assessments (self or circle) indicate that you have room for improvement in the area of leader credibility *and* you are also finding disparity between your responses and the authors' options, chances are you will find growth by working through these exercises and the accompanying readings. However, be reminded, this will not happen overnight. Growing your leadership intelligence is a worthy endeavor but is a painstakingly time-consuming undertaking. It requires the rewiring of learning patterns that are ingrained in your most innate thought processes and this takes time. (See appendix B for a graphic representation.)

On the other hand, if you find your solutions and the solutions offered in the "Authors' Options" coincide to a great degree yet your "self" score is lower than the mean for the group shown at the end of your LSI assessment for credibility, one of two things is happening. Either you are lacking in self-confidence yet your decision making is solid or, conversely, perhaps you are somewhat overconfident but nonetheless making good decisions.

If the first is the case, working through the scenarios should enhance your self-confidence. The second option (overconfidence) is the one to be most wary of. Leaders in this category many times find themselves derailed as leaders, even though they generally are good decision makers. Working through the scenarios should help to instill the idea that there is more than one acceptable solution to most problems and issues and thus lessen one potential major consequence of overconfidence—the feeling that you have the only viable solution.

If you opt to have a circle or 360-assessment done and find that your solutions and the solutions offered in the "Authors' Options" coincide for the most part and yet your circle scores are outside the standard deviation (available from the LSI team when a circle or 360-assessment is done) LSI for credibility, it is possible that a different set of problems is occurring. Perhaps you are selecting the course of action you believe is best for the scenario but, in reality, you would not implement it, or perhaps the problem is one of *perception*. It is much more likely that it is the former, but in rare instances, perception can be the cause of low scores in credibility. This could be a case of projection; for example, you may not "look" credible. You will recall from the chapter on credibility in *Leadership Intelligence: Navigating to your True North* that mention was made of how "what you wear" infers or projects an image. Such could be the case in this instance.

Finally, improving your leadership intelligence and "adaptive capacity," as stated in the preface, is a process. As you will recall, the notion of leadership intelligence is predicated on the theory that there is a genetic predisposition toward leadership.

As Marquis and Tilcsik[1] so aptly noted, imprinting may take place during brief sensitive periods of high susceptibility during the formative process, during the teachable moment, or at yet another time of susceptibility, and that, once established, imprints are persistent.

The lessons in this book are to be utilized to grow LSI in this third way—over the long, repetitive process. To that end and to truly be imprinted with any of the competencies, actions for building the various skill sets may be found in appendix C.

True credibility is only gained by congruence of words and actions.

MEDICALLY INCOMPETENT

You have been asked by a colleague and dear friend for help with a pending university-wide accreditation visit. He has been diagnosed with terminal cancer and will likely not survive long enough to be present at the time of the visit. He has gotten approval from his boss for you to assist with the work ahead.

Over the coming months, your colleague's health begins to deteriorate. However, he continues to refer to the job as his "legacy" and drags himself to work nearly daily. It is the most important "last" thing he will accomplish in this lifetime.

The time has come to "take over" the project as your colleague is not only desperately ill but his mind has also become weak with the continued chemotherapy regimen. There have been a few times recently you have broached "taking over" with him and he has stonewalled you. The university vice president responsible for the visit is inquiring regarding his ability to continue.

What do you do?

_____
_____
_____
_____
_____
_____
_____

Suggested Reading

Green and Leonard, *Leadership Intelligence: Navigating to Your True North*, p. 26.

Additional Selected Reading

Ehrich, L., N. Cranston, M. Kimber, and K. Starr. (Un)ethical Practices and Ethical Dilemmas in Universities: Academic Leaders' Perceptions. *International Studies in Educational Administration* 40(2) (January 2012): 99–114.

CHAPTER 1

SMALL THINGS MATTER

One of the small pleasures of your work day has always been the morning coffee break. On your new job, it comes at about 10:00 a.m. The campus coffee shop is where students and staff have a cup of "joe" and more importantly have the chance to interact in a more casual setting. The campus coffee house does not fall under your purview as Director of Student Life but is overseen by your supervisor, the head of the Student Services Department.

A short walk takes you to the coffee shop, which today is empty except for the counter attendant, a few students seated at a table, and one professor who is in line ahead of you. The professor pays for his coffee and takes a seat at a nearby table.

As you approach the counter the attendant says, "Hi, aren't you Dr. Smith, the new Director of Student Life?"

"Why, yes, I am," you reply. "And your name is?"

He answers, "James. James Jones."

"Good to meet you James. I'd like a cup of coffee, a grande if you have the larger sizes. And please leave room for cream."

James retrieves a grande cup and begins filling it. It smells delicious and whets your appetite for the coffee even more. As he passes the cup of coffee to you he says, "This one's on the house."

What should you do?

_____
_____
_____
_____
_____
_____
_____

Suggested Reading

Green and Leonard, *Leadership Intelligence: Navigating to Your True North*, p. 28.

Additional Selected Reading

Gentile, M. How to Challenge Unethical Behavior at Work—and Prevail. *Harvard Business Review* (March 2010): 114–117.

EXCEPTION TO THE RULE

"Rules were made to be broken" is the old adage that we hear time and again, especially when we feel the need to break one. But are rules made to be broken? Or were they made because someone "went too far" when there was no rule?

Exam day is a day set by faculty or perhaps by other authorities at an institution. Nonetheless, conflicts with those dates oftentimes arise. On occasion, there are legitimate reasons for making exceptions to these dates. Does making an exception for one cause the proverbial "barn door" to open on exceptions for others?

A student in the graduate program oversees accreditation for her school. The dates of the visit conflict with the semester exam finals. The faculty member refuses to allow the student to take the exam at a different time. The student has come to you as department chair for help.

What do you do?

_____
_____
_____
_____
_____
_____
_____
_____

Suggested Reading

Green and Leonard, *Leadership Intelligence: Navigating to Your True North*, p. 29.

Additional Selected Reading

Broadbelt, G. What Is Responsible Leadership? *Training Journal* (October 2015): 41–45.

CHAPTER 1

A HELPING HAND

As the new Director of Student Life, you want to be involved in as many student activities as possible without seeming to micromanage or interfere with the Student Activities Coordinator who reports to you. You schedule a meeting with him to discuss this issue.

What should you say?

_____

_____

_____

_____

_____

_____

_____

Suggested Reading

Green and Leonard, *Leadership Intelligence: Navigating to Your True North*, p. 30.

Additional Selected Reading

Gross, K. Truth, Transparency and Trust: Treasured Values in Higher Education. *New England Journal of Higher Education* 1 (February 2015).

FAILURE TO LAUNCH

As a faculty member in higher education, promotions are few and far between. An assistant professor must work for five years prior to being eligible for promotion to associate professor. Generally speaking, the same is true for an associate professor working toward the rank of full professor. Tenure in higher education, however, is an entirely separate issue with collegiality being a large part of granting this status. The promotion review process is a year-long one and goes through a voting protocol at the departmental, college, and university levels along with soliciting additional remarks from the department chair, dean, and provost.

Phil is a good colleague and faculty member. He is likeable, a good teacher, and especially supportive of new faculty. However, when it comes to publishing, your assessment as chair is that he doesn't quite make the mark. His departmental colleagues, however, have reviewed his materials and passed him along for promotion with a 5–4 vote. As chair of the department, you are expected to write the next letter. Not only do you believe he hasn't done what is necessary, you have served on the college tenure committee for many years. You are confident he will not pass the expectations of that committee.

Prior to writing your letter, protocol requires you to bring him in to discuss his progress thus far in the process. You know he will be pleased to receive the news he has passed the departmental vote regardless of the vote count.

What will you say to Phil?

_____
_____
_____
_____
_____
_____
_____

Suggested Reading

Green and Leonard, *Leadership Intelligence: Navigating to Your True North*, p. 31.

Additional Selected Reading

Jenkins, R. What Makes a Good Leader? *Chronicle of Higher Education* (February 2013): A43.

CHAPTER 1

A BOND IS FORMED

Trust is relational. It is a reciprocal process that is built over time but always starts with sharing. That sharing may be directed at a delegated responsibility, a mutual responsibility or event, a communication, or some other interaction between two individuals. Trust is built when each individual carries out their agreed-upon responsibilities and/or handles the event or communication in the anticipated manner. Or, if the intended outcome cannot be achieved, communication occurs that provides a plausible explanation for the failure to follow through.

As a leader, one of the first lessons that you learn is that openness, transparency, and frank communication lend themselves to building trust. These practices are especially important to a new leader or a leader who is new to a situation as they help to build a bond not only of trust but also of respect between the leader and the organization's members and constituents.

On becoming the Director of Student Life, it is critical to both short-term and long-term success that you start immediately to build a bond of trust and respect with college personnel, most notably the deans, department chairs, directors, and coordinators (though all are important). As you become more familiar with your department, it becomes obvious that the coordinators have played a limited role in hiring. You want to expand that role and tell them that you will only interview candidates that they wish to recommend.

Moreover, unless some negative information arises, you will endorse their candidates for approval. However, as a caveat to that process, you tell them as well that they will be responsible for terminating any candidate they select who fails to perform. The first openings come, and the Housing Coordinator has cleared posting the vacancies with you and is set to begin interviews.

What should you do?

_____
_____
_____
_____
_____

Suggested Reading

Green and Leonard, *Leadership Intelligence: Navigating to Your True North*, p. 32.

Additional Selected Reading

Horton, H. Thirteen Traits of Effective Leaders. AU-24, *Concepts for Air Force Leadership* (2016). Retrieved from http://www.au.af.mil/au/awc/awcgate/au-24/horton.pdf.

AUTHORS' OPTIONS FOR CREDIBILITY-BASED SJTS

MEDICALLY INCOMPETENT

A. Talk to your friend, again, but this time let him know that the boss is inquiring about his ability to stay on as project director. Suggest it may be time to step down.
B. Explain to his boss that based on your interactions you do not believe he is competent to continue; however, you would appreciate consideration for keeping him onboard as long as is feasible for the organization.
C. Explain to his boss that based on your interactions you do not believe he is competent to continue.
D. Tell his boss that you are not comfortable giving information regarding your friend's mental (working) capacity.
E. Other option: _____
_____
_____

SMALL THINGS MATTER

A. Take the coffee and thank him for the kindness.
B. Take the coffee and put an appropriate tip in the tip jar.
C. Take and pay for the coffee as the professor ahead of you paid.
D. Take the coffee and tell the department head how nice a gesture that was when you see her.

E. Other option: _____

_____

_____

EXCEPTION TO THE RULE

A. Allow the student to take the exam at a different time and tell the faculty member you have done so.
B. Meet with the faculty member and discuss the possibility of another option.
C. Explain to the student that although you are sympathetic, the established dates are the faculty member's prerogative.
D. Suggest to the student that they take the matter up with the dean as this is a very difficult faculty member whom you have had no success with in the past.
E. Other option: _____

_____

_____

A HELPING HAND

A. "Being new here, I would really like to get a feel for the activities the students are involved with. We both have very full schedules. It would help both of us if you would allow me to attend some of the activities in your place. But if you are not comfortable with that, I understand. What do you think?"
B. "Being new here, I would really like to get a feel for the activities the students are involved with. Your schedule is very full. I intend to attend as many of the events as I can. I will let you know when I intend to come so you can stay home and take some time off."
C. "Being new here, I would really like to get a feel for the activities the students are involved with. We both have full schedules but it would help me if you would allow me to attend some of the activities in your place."
D. "Being new here, I would really like to get a feel for the activities the students are involved with. Your schedule is very full. Would it help you if I attended some of the activities in your place?"
E. Other option: _____

_____

_____

AUTHORS' OPTIONS FOR CREDIBILITY-BASED SJTS

FAILURE TO LAUNCH

A. Remind Phil that a pass at the department level is just the beginning. Tell Phil you will write a letter of support but that it is no guarantee of promotion.
B. Remind Phil that a pass at the department level is just the beginning. Recommend to Phil that he withdraw his materials prior to your writing a letter of nonsupport.
C. Remind Phil that a pass at the department level is just the beginning. Explain to Phil the reasons you cannot write a letter of support and allow Phil to determine his next course of action, reminding him that he has full right to proceed if he would like to do so; if he decides to move forward, write the letter of nonsupport.
D. Remind Phil that a pass at the department level is just the beginning. Explain to Phil the reasons you cannot write a letter of support but encourage him to go forward. He might just get better results at the college level; you never know about office politics.
E. Other option: _____

_____

_____

A BOND IS FORMED

A. Allow the interviews to proceed without comment.
B. Allow the interviews but tell him you want to see the applications to mark those who seem best-suited.
C. Return applications but mark one specific candidate as eminently acceptable.
D. Tell him to postpone the interviews pending further discussion.
E. Allow the interviews but ask him whether he knows someone else who might want to apply.
F. Other option: _____

_____

_____

3

LESSONS ON COMPETENCE

Professional competence requires constant renewal. Higher education leaders, whether at public or private or proprietary junior/community colleges or four-year colleges or universities, come from a variety of backgrounds. Some rise through the ranks in higher education while others join the ranks of higher education leaders (especially upper echelon leaders such as presidents, provosts, or specialists in accounting, or athletics, for example) from areas outside higher education.

Regardless of the path to leadership, these individuals must master their trade and doing so requires constant renewal and an unwavering devotion to lifelong learning. The credo of higher education leaders, like that of leaders in all areas, should be that they will remain current and thoroughly knowledgeable in their field—that they will be competent in their chosen field.

The scenarios in this chapter are, in one way or another, related to a leader's competence. If your LSI assessment scores indicated this as an area for needed growth, you should work through the scenarios with a couple of things in mind. First, take particular note of the "Authors' Options" section, which provides responses to each problem at the end of each chapter of SJTs.

In working through the scenarios and reviewing the "Authors' Options," one of two things will happen. You will find disparity between your responses and those of the authors, or you might, indeed, find that your responses coincide with the authors' (see appendix B for a graphic representation). Next, reflect on the information you gained from the LSI assessment. If you acknowledge that competence is an area for growth based on the assessment, ask yourself if this was based on your self-assessment, the circle assessment, or both.

If either or both assessments (self or circle) indicate that you have room for improvement in the area of leader competence *and* you are also finding disparity between your responses and the authors' options, chances are you will find growth via working through these exercises and accompanying readings. However, be reminded, this will not happen overnight. Growing your leadership intelligence is a worthy endeavor, but is a painstakingly time-consuming undertaking. It requires rewiring of learning patterns that are ingrained in your most innate thought processes and this takes time. (See appendix B for a graphic representation.)

On the other hand, if you find your solutions and the solutions offered in the "Authors' Options" coincide to a great degree yet your "self" score is lower than the mean for the group shown at the end of your LSI assessment for competence, one of two things is happening. Either you are lacking in self-confidence yet your decision making is solid or, conversely, perhaps you are somewhat overconfident but nonetheless making good decisions.

If the first is the case, working through the scenarios should enhance your self-confidence. The second option (overconfidence) is the one to be most wary of. Leaders in this category many times find themselves derailed as leaders, even though they generally are good decision makers. Working through the scenarios should help to instill the idea that there is more than one acceptable solution to most problems and issues and thus lessen one potential major consequence of overconfidence—the feeling that you have the only viable solution.

If you opt to have a circle or 360-assessment done and find that your solutions and the solutions offered in the "Authors' Options" coincide for the most part and yet your circle scores are outside the standard deviation (available from the LSI team when a circle or 360-assessment is done) LSI for competence, it is possible that a different set of problems is occurring. Perhaps you are selecting the course of action you believe is best for the scenario but, in reality, you would not implement it, or perhaps the problem is one of *perception*. It is much more likely that it is the former, but in rare instances, perception can be the cause of low scores in competence. This could be a case of projection; for example, you may not "look" credible. You will recall from the chapter on credibility in *Leadership Intelligence: Navigating to your True North* that mention was made of how "what you wear" infers or projects an image. Such could be the case in this instance.

Finally, improving your leadership intelligence and "adaptive capacity," as stated in the preface, is a process. As you will recall, the notion of leadership intelligence is predicated on the theory that there is a genetic predisposition toward leadership.

As Marquis and Tilcsik[1] so aptly noted, imprinting may take place during brief sensitive periods of high susceptibility during the formative process, during the teachable moment, or at yet another time of susceptibility, and that, once established, imprints are persistent.

The lessons in this book are to be utilized to grow LSI in this third way—over the long, repetitive process. To that end and to truly be imprinted with any of the competencies, actions for building the various skill sets may be found in appendix C.

Again, quoting *Leadership Intelligence: Navigating to Your True North*—"true competence in effectively applying 'hard skills' requires mastery of 'soft skills'—that is, people-centered skills."

HOW MUCH IS ENOUGH?

Earning promotion in academia at the university is generally a long and arduous process. At most institutions, the journey from beginning assistant professor to associate professor includes a span of six years of time and jumping through a few hoops. In some institutions, the "hoops" are clearly delineated; at others, the rite of passage is more obscure. Some believe it is this way for political purposes, others so that judgment may be employed.

As academic dean of the college, you are tasked with oversight and evaluation of the promotion dossiers that work themselves through the college. Lily Smith is one of several assistant professors who have submitted materials through the proper channels for evaluation, aspiring to the rank of associate professor. Having passed promotion rigor at both the departmental and college levels, it is your responsibility now to review Dr. Smith's dossier.

As you begin going through her materials, you notice that although she has *many* publications, a *huge* number of them are editorial. As a matter of fact, the majority of them are editorial *and* very brief. You do find one of the publications to be noteworthy, but this one is the only one and it is dually authored. Your position as dean is relatively new, yet you are aware that Dr. Smith is well-liked by the peers in her department. You are also aware that, historically, the college vote aligns with the departmental one—regardless.

Although Dr. Smith may have met the minimum number of publications required to pass promotion muster, the quality of her work leaves much to be desired.

What will your decision be?

_____

_____

_____

_____

_____

_____

Suggested Reading

Green and Leonard, *Leadership Intelligence: Navigating to Your True North*, p. 38.

Additional Selected Reading

Fryer, B. Timeless Leadership. *Harvard Business Review* (March 2008): 45–49.

CHAPTER 3

LEADERSHIP ORIENTATION

Being perceived as and feeling individually that you are competent is vital to leader success. To this end, higher education leaders, like competent leaders in all fields, impact the perceptions of others by the way they behave, act, and speak. Behaviors, actions, and utterances exemplify the leader's level of competence to organizational members and constituents. But how can a leader come to understand how he or she is perceived? One way to gain insight into how one is perceived is through 360-evaluative feedback.

In combination with that feedback, it is vital that a leader individually be consistently reflective personally and professionally. That reflective process allows a leader to understand who they are and what they stand for as a leader and defines their leadership competence. That competence is one characteristic that tends to set them apart as a leader, to make them discernible. And competence is often the key to both long-term and short-term success as a leader.

A list of characteristics often associated with effective leadership in higher education is provided below. Rate each item below on a scale of 1 to 10 (with 1 indicating the lowest importance and 10 the highest) in relation to the item's importance in displaying leadership competence. A scoring rubric is provided in the "Authors' Options" section at the end of the chapter.[2]

1	Establish principles of treating people	1	2	3	4	5	6	7	8	9	10
2	Foster collaboration	1	2	3	4	5	6	7	8	9	10
3	Seek opportunities to make changes	1	2	3	4	5	6	7	8	9	10
4	Envision the future with a unique image	1	2	3	4	5	6	7	8	9	10
5	Keep hope and determination alive	1	2	3	4	5	6	7	8	9	10
6	Experiment and take risks	1	2	3	4	5	6	7	8	9	10
7	Set standards of excellence	1	2	3	4	5	6	7	8	9	10
8	Get people to see exciting possibilities	1	2	3	4	5	6	7	8	9	10
9	Recognize individuals' contributions	1	2	3	4	5	6	7	8	9	10
10	Build team spirit	1	2	3	4	5	6	7	8	9	10
11	Breathe life into the (organizational) vision	1	2	3	4	5	6	7	8	9	10
12	Share rewards within the team	1	2	3	4	5	6	7	8	9	10
13	Actively involve others	1	2	3	4	5	6	7	8	9	10
14	Create opportunities for success	1	2	3	4	5	6	7	8	9	10
15	Accept mistakes, disappointments, and failures as opportunities to learn	1	2	3	4	5	6	7	8	9	10

Table based on the work of Simon Black (see endnote 2).

Suggested Reading

Green and Leonard, *Leadership Intelligence: Navigating to Your True North*, p. 39.

Additional Selected Reading

Frangos, C. How Cisco Gets Brutally Honest Feedback to Top Leaders. *Harvard Business Review* (December 2015): 2–4.

CHAPTER 3

YOU'RE NOT THE BOSS OF ME

You are the new chair of the department—appointed—which, in and of itself, does not necessarily set a good tone for the other faculty in the department. Nonetheless, it is what it is. You are determined to make the best of an unusual situation so you have an open-door policy and are willing to hear anyone's concerns, thoughts, and/or ideas.

Your first faculty meeting is forthcoming so you send out an "all-call" for items the members would like to see on the agenda. A couple of innocuous items are forwarded to you and you add them to the agenda. Rumor, however, has it that one of the more outspoken faculty members is preparing to wreak havoc at the upcoming meeting. The morning of the faculty meeting, you are told that she and a few others met over coffee the night before to determine how to undermine you at the meeting this morning.

Although a bit anxious, you head to the meeting with a positive attitude. You run into the alleged troublemaker outside the meeting hallway. She is extremely friendly and you greet her confidently; the two of you walk into the room together. You pass out the agenda and begin the meeting. Everything seems to be going well as there is good dialogue among the faculty. The meeting is near closure and you thank everyone for their input and attendance. Before you can react, the rogue faculty member stands up and says, "I know we are near the end of the meeting so I would like to ask all tenured faculty to stay for a few minutes so we can discuss the unusual appointment of our new chair."

What do you do?

_____

_____

_____

_____

_____

_____

_____

Suggested Reading

Green and Leonard, *Leadership Intelligence: Navigating to Your True North*, p. 41.

Additional Suggested Reading

Toegel, G., and J.-L. Barsoux. How to Preempt Team Conflict. *Harvard Business Review* (June 2016): 79–83.

SEE AND BE SEEN

A week has passed since you became Director of Student Life at a small denominational college and it has been a whirlwind of a week—meeting people, attending meetings, and working hard to get a feel for the organization and how it works.

Toward the end of the week, however, things are beginning to settle down and you have time to reflect on the imperatives the head of the Student Services Department has set out for you. Those imperatives include visiting the Head Resident Advisers weekly or more often as needed, overseeing the Student Union, overseeing the work of the Student Activities Coordinator, overseeing chapel attendance, and overseeing the work of the Housing Director.

The students have arrived on campus and the semester has begun in earnest. The dorms are bustling, the Student Union is full, the coffee shop is filled to capacity, the book store is swamped, and the first chapel is next week.

What should your plan be for next week?

_____
_____
_____
_____
_____
_____
_____

Suggested Reading

Green and Leonard, *Leadership Intelligence: Navigating to Your True North*, p. 42.

Additional Selected Reading

Beattie, J., B. Thornton, R. Laden, and D. Brackett. 21st Century Challenges in Higher Education: Strategic Changes and Unintended Consequences. *NCPEA International Journal of Educational Leadership Preparation* 8(1) (March 2013): 62–71.

CHAPTER 3

YELLING

Over the past couple of years, your assistant chair has become your best friend. She is a hard worker, energetic, and full of exciting ideas. You are very pleased she is a part of your team and you are quick to encourage and support her. As you reflect on it, actually, your entire staff is incredible. They comprise a good team, always willing to support you and each other. The office runs very well.

After a long day of meetings at the dean's office, you return to the building to find most everyone has headed home. However, you notice that Mary Martin, the administrative assistant, is still here. As you are walking to your office, you peek into her space and inquire about the day.

Surprisingly, Mary seems troubled. She tells you that during the course of the day, the assistant chair called your budget coordinator in with some questions. The next thing she heard was yelling by the assistant chair and the budget coordinator left in tears. Mary was shocked by the assistant chair's behavior.

What do you do?

Suggested Reading

Green and Leonard, *Leadership Intelligence: Navigating to Your True North*, p. 44.

Additional Selected Reading

Bryman, A. Effective Leadership in Higher Education: A Literature Review. *Studies in Higher Education* 32(6) (2007): 693–710.

IF IT *IS* BROKEN, FIX IT

Even a small student center seems to demand constant attention. Pool cues, treadmills, televisions, even chairs and sometimes the heating and air conditioning units break and fail. But beyond those unfortunate occurrences, there are more problematic issues of staffing with student workers, maintaining efficient communication with those workers, and limiting use of the facility to authorized students and staff.

As Director of Student Life, those challenges surface quickly after your appointment. Those three problems (regular maintenance, staffing, and communication) combine to produce a fourth problem—complaints by students about not being able to use the facility. The budget is limited.

What should you do?

_____
_____
_____
_____
_____
_____
_____
_____

Suggested Reading

Green and Leonard, *Leadership Intelligence: Navigating to Your True North*, p. 46.

Additional Selected Reading

Dyer, G., and M. Dyer. Strategic Leadership for Sustainability by Higher Education: The American College and University Presidents' Climate Commitment. *Journal of Cleaner Production* 140(1) (January 2017): 111–116. Retrieved from http://www.sciencedirect.com/science/article/pii/S0959652615011683.

CHAPTER 3

ERASING 100 "ATTA-BOYS"

In the South, there are lots of colloquialisms. One of them goes something like this . . . one "ole shoot" can erase 100 "atta-boys." The thought behind this phrase is that either a) you can work very hard for a long time to build a good reputation and one misstep can do great damage to all that work, or b) similarly, you can believe strongly in someone based on built trust or work ethic and that can be demolished with one willful act of poor judgment.

This was the case when the department chair sent out a professional performance evaluation to her faculty. At the end of the spring term, the chair sent a request for feedback to improve her performance for the following year. She assured the faculty the anonymous evaluations would not be reviewed until the summer break was underway.

As she began to open the sealed envelopes and review the feedback, she felt pretty good that a positive year had evolved. It was at that moment that she opened the "offending" one. In an instant, all of the "atta-boys" were erased.

How should the chair react?

_____

_____

_____

_____

_____

_____

_____

Suggested Reading

Green and Leonard, *Leadership Intelligence: Navigating to Your True North*, p. 46.

Additional Selected Reading

Banta, T. Accentuating the Positive in Our Work. *Assessment Update* (April 7, 2014). Retrieved from http://www.assessmentupdate.com/sample-articles/accentuating-the-positive-in-our-work.aspx.

4

AUTHORS' OPTIONS FOR COMPETENCE-BASED SJTS

HOW MUCH IS ENOUGH?

A. Based on your review, the dossier clearly is insufficient; approve Dr. Smith but correct the matter prior to the next round (year) of promotions.
B. Based on your review, the dossier clearly is insufficient; make an appointment with Dr. Smith to discuss your analysis of the materials and offer her a chance to withdraw them rather than forcing you to deny her promotion.
C. Based on your review, the dossier clearly is insufficient; write a succinct memo (on letterhead) to this effect with your denial of approval. Send materials along with the others that are up for promotion on to the next reviewing body.
D. Based on your review, the dossier clearly is insufficient; contact the department chair for a conference regarding the lack of substance so she might reconvene the departmental committee.
E. Other option: _____
_____
_____

LEADERSHIP ORIENTATION

Enter your rating for each item in the "Leadership Orientation Chart" on the next page. Then, enter these scores in the scoring rubric for leadership orientation in the "Authors' Solutions" to SJTs section.

CHAPTER 4

1 ___	2 ___	3 ___	4 ___	5 ___
6 ___	7 ___	8 ___	9 ___	10 ___
11 ___	12 ___	13 ___	14 ___	15 ___

YOU'RE NOT THE BOSS OF ME

A. Tell them there will be no meeting unless you are present also.
B. Tell the faculty that there will be no "meeting after the meeting" and ask them to go forward with their otherwise scheduled business.
C. Stand at the door until everyone else has left so you can see who exactly comprises this group (and so they can see you are noticing this fact).
D. Carry on as if the remark had not been made.
E. Other option: _____

_____

_____

SEE AND BE SEEN

A. Talk with the department head to see what her specific priorities are.
B. Set a schedule leading up to and following chapel that will have you visiting all of your assigned areas of responsibility.
C. Chapel is a prime activity. Make sure that goes well and attend to the other areas next week.
D. Require the Student Activities Coordinator and Housing Director to schedule general meetings with their groups and go over the agenda items you want them to cover.
E. Other option: _____

_____

_____

AUTHORS' OPTIONS FOR COMPETENCE-BASED SJTS

YELLING

A. Invite your assistant chair in for a visit first thing in the morning. Inquire about the incident and the yelling. Admonish your assistant chair in a professional manner and ask her to apologize to the coordinator.
B. Invite your assistant chair in for a visit first thing in the morning. Use the teachable moment to correct the assistant chair's behavior. Have her assure you this will not happen again.
C. Invite your assistant chair in for a visit first thing in the morning. Have formal documentation of the incident available for the assistant chair to sign after your conference.
D. Invite your assistant chair in first thing in the morning. Ask if Mary's assessment of the situation was correct. Ask her what the coordinator did to provoke her.
E. Other option: _____

_____

_____

IF IT *IS* BROKEN, FIX IT

A. Meet with the workers and make sure they understand that they must check IDs and report broken equipment. Then monitor the results.
B. Meet with the workers and tell them that if they fail to check IDs and report broken equipment, they will be fired.
C. Secure permission and appoint student managers to oversee the student workers and charge the managers with the responsibility of reporting broken equipment and checking IDs.
D. Meet with the head of the Student Services Department and ask her advice.
E. Other option: _____

_____

_____

ERASING 100 "ATTA-BOYS"

A. Rather than internalizing the one negative evaluation, the leader should take the feedback as an opportunity to improve in a particular area.

B. The leader should ignore the negative evaluation and still consider herself as having received an "A" for the year.
C. The leader has worked hard for an entire year in all areas. If some of the teachers do not appreciate that, perhaps she should find another school.
D. The leader has worked hard for an entire year in all areas. If some of the teachers do not appreciate that, perhaps they should find another school.
E. Other option: _____
_____
_____

5

LESSONS ON THE ABILITY TO INSPIRE

When our intent as leaders is to inspire, we often fall short of our goal. For some reason, as leaders, we believe that inspiration is some mystical or magical force that only coaches and motivational speakers possess. Although inspiration can sometimes include such elements as high energy and mountain-moving motivation, inspiration is best achieved through what we do and say.

The scenarios in this chapter are, in one way or another, related to a leader's ability to inspire. If your LSI assessment scores indicate this as an area for needed growth, you should work through the scenarios with a couple of things in mind. First, take particular note of the "Authors' Options" section, which provides responses to each problem at the end of each chapter of SJTs.

In working through the scenarios and reviewing the "Authors' Options," one of two things will happen. You will find disparity between your responses and those of the authors, or you might, indeed, find that your responses coincide with the authors' (see appendix B for a graphic representation). Next, reflect on the information you gained from the LSI assessment. If you acknowledge that ability to inspire is an area for growth based on the assessment, ask yourself if this was based on your self-assessment, the circle assessment, or both.

If either or both assessments (self or circle) indicate that you have room for improvement in the area of leader ability to inspire *and* you are also finding disparity between your responses and the authors' options, chances are you will find growth by working through these exercises and the accompanying readings. However, be reminded, this will not happen overnight. Growing your leadership intelligence is a worthy endeavor but is a painstakingly time-consuming undertaking. It requires the rewiring of learning patterns that are ingrained in your most innate thought processes and this takes time. (See appendix B for a graphic representation.)

On the other hand, if you find your solutions and the solutions offered in the "Authors' Options" coincide to a great degree yet your "self" score is lower than the mean for the group shown at the end of your LSI assessment for ability to inspire, one of two things is happening. Either you are lacking in self-confidence yet your decision making is solid or, conversely, perhaps you are somewhat overconfident but nonetheless making good decisions.

If the first is the case, working through the scenarios should enhance your self-confidence. The second option (overconfidence) is the one to be most wary of. Leaders in this category many times find themselves derailed as leaders, even though they generally are good decision makers. Working through the scenarios should help to instill the idea that there is more than one acceptable solution to most problems and issues and thus lessen one potential major consequence of overconfidence—the feeling that you have the only viable solution.

If you opt to have a circle or 360-assessment done and find that your solutions and the solutions offered in the "Authors' Options" coincide for the most part and yet your circle scores are outside the standard deviation (available from the LSI team when a circle or 360-assessment is done) LSI for ability to inspire, it is possible that a different set of problems is occurring. Perhaps you are selecting the course of action you believe is best for the scenario but, in reality, you would not implement it, or perhaps the problem is one of *perception*. It is much more likely that it is the former, but in rare instances, perception can be the cause of low scores in ability to inspire. This could be a case of projection; for example, you may not "look" credible. You will recall from the chapter on credibility in *Leadership Intelligence: Navigating to your True North* that mention was made of how "what you wear" infers or projects an image. Such could be the case in this instance.

Finally, improving your leadership intelligence and "adaptive capacity," as stated in the preface, is a process. As you will recall, the notion of leadership intelligence is predicated on the theory that there is a genetic predisposition toward leadership.

As Marquis and Tilcsik[1] so aptly noted, imprinting may take place during brief sensitive periods of high susceptibility during the formative process, during the teachable moment, or at yet another time of susceptibility, and that, once established, imprints are persistent.

The lessons in this book are to be utilized to grow LSI in this third way—over the long, repetitive process. To that end and to truly be imprinted with any of the competencies, actions for building the various skill sets may be found in appendix C.

"True inspiration for both the leader and peers and followers comes from within by finding value and meaning in the work they do."[2]

GET RID OF THE LEADERSHIP CLASS

You are the new department chair of a program in Educational Leadership. One of the mandates with which you were charged was to organize the program prior to the impending accreditation visit. It has been several years since the curriculum has been aligned; furthermore, several adjuncts are teaching in the program and are not aware of the standards required by the various accrediting bodies. It is time to pull the faculty together and give everything a close review.

The faculty is all in attendance and ready to divide and conquer. You assign different duties to different groups with the intention of regrouping and sharing accomplishments prior to lunch. Things seem to be running smoothly. When the large group reconvenes, discussion is underway regarding the curriculum. The biggest concern for the group is that it appears there are no mandated core courses that all students must take.

Although this is a surprising revelation, the group is clearly pleased to have identified this foundational issue and is ready to create a core of required courses for the program. A laundry list of courses that are currently taught are identified and outlined for everyone to review. It appears there are more courses than core. The group must reduce the core offerings by one class.

The newest hire to the department, for whom many in the group have little regard, has been relatively quiet up to this point. There is much banter back and forth between the more seasoned, and incidentally more vested, faculty members about which courses MUST remain and which might be acceptable to remove. It is evident the new assistant professor has disconnected from the dialogue.

Just before the lunch break, and during more rhetoric regarding the value of certain courses, the new professor raises his hand. You are excited to see that he has an opinion. With no sarcasm intended, when you recognize him, he shares, "Why don't we just remove one of those two leadership classes? After all, this is a leadership program. They should already know that stuff."

Silence drops over the group.

What do you do?

_____

_____

_____

Suggested Reading

Green and Leonard, *Leadership Intelligence: Navigating to Your True North*, p. 52.

Additional Selected Reading

Cottringer, W. Light Their Fires. *Supervision* 76(9) (September 2015): 6.

CHAPTER 5

FRATERNITY DAYS

You heard a rumor this morning that a group of students has created or continued an unofficial fraternity or club in one of the dorms and has been playing pranks on the residents. In conversation with the head of a department, she confirms that this has gone on in the past and has had to be quashed. You talk to the Head Resident Assistant and he has heard the rumor too but does not know who is involved.

What should you do?

_____

_____

_____

Suggested Reading

Green and Leonard, *Leadership Intelligence: Navigating to Your True North*, p. 32.

Additional Selected Reading

Welbourne, T. Taking the Pulse of Leaders to Optimize and Direct Employee Energy at Work. *Wiley Online Library: Employee Relations Today* 41 (March 2014): 1–9. DOI 10.1002/ert.21437.

NOT MY JOB

Group classroom assignments are frequently made at the graduate level. In the "teamwork" world we all are now a part of, the ability to establish roles and fulfill them is critical. Regardless, it seems that someone is always unhappy when *classroom* teamwork is assigned. One person takes over, another person "rides the group," a third person is always late or does sloppy work. The list of "reasons" NOT to work in classroom teams or groups is unending.

In the following scenario in a leadership program, a classroom team is assigned at the beginning of the semester. This team will work together throughout the semester on several projects. One of the group members contracts a very serious illness about halfway through the semester that limits his ability to fully participate.

How should the other group members respond?

_____

_____

_____

Suggested Reading

Green and Leonard, *Leadership Intelligence: Navigating to Your True North*, p. 55.

Additional Selected Reading

DeClercq, D., and I. Belausteguigoitia. Overcoming the Dark Side of Task Conflict: Buffering Roles of Transformational Leadership, Tenacity, and Passion for Work. *European Management Journal* 35(1) (February 2017): 78–90.

CHAPTER 5

A ROSE BY ANY OTHER NAME

Your secretary tells you for what seems like the hundredth time that Dr. Ambrose "did it this way." Whatever it is, your predecessor had a way to do it, he had been there for many years, and the way it had always been done worked just fine. Similar remarks have been made by the Housing Coordinator and the Coordinator of Student Activities, though not with as great a frequency. You have taken these comments with as much grace as possible out of respect for them and your predecessor, but your patience is wearing thin with this one, constant reminder.

What should you say to those who approach you with those comments?

_____

_____

_____

Suggested Reading

Green and Leonard, *Leadership Intelligence: Navigating to Your True North*, p. 59.

Additional Selected Reading

Nguyen, Q., J. Kuntz, K. Näswall, and S. Malinen. Employee Resilience and Leadership Styles: The Moderating Role of Proactive Personality and Optimism. *New Zealand Journal of Psychology* 45(2) (August 2016): 13–20.

DEFINE "NASTY"

Some of the most important people at the university are the graduate assistants (GAs). The university thrives on the creation of new knowledge and much of that work comes off the backs of the graduate assistants the institution employs. Although the GAs generally take away more than they are asked to do, it is definitely a symbiotic relationship.

Your administrative assistant knocks and tells you that one of the college GAs would like to meet with you. Although there is a mountain of paperwork on your desk, you push it aside and invite the GA in for a brief conversation. The GA immediately begins to tell you how poorly her assigned faculty member has been treating her. The behavior borders on workplace harassment. You thank the GA for having the courage to share the information with you and then assure her you will investigate.

At the next available opportunity, you send for the offending faculty member. This full professor seems concerned about the fact that you have sent for him. After initial pleasantries, you inquire whether the professor might be having difficulties with his assigned graduate assistant. The faculty member hesitates to respond and asks for clarification of the problem.

You respond, "I have received a complaint that your behavior toward Ms. Jordan has become nasty. Would you agree with that?"

The professor then responds, "Well, that would depend on how you define nasty."

How do you respond?

_____

_____

_____

Suggested Reading

Green and Leonard, *Leadership Intelligence: Navigating to Your True North*, p. 60.

Additional Selected Reading

Carucci, R. Organizations Can't Change If Leaders Can't Change with Them. *Harvard Business Review: Change Management* (October 2016). Retrieved from https://hbr.org/2016/10/organizations-cant-change-if-leaders-cant-change-with-them.

CHAPTER 5

PUBLISH OR PERISH

Well, you've done it. You've finally been awarded that elusive doctorate and you are on top of the world. You have sacrificed (as has your family) for what seemed like forever. Now you are on the other side of "the dream." You have led as a building-level school principal and now it's time to get out there and change the world.

Fast-forward one year. Congratulations! You did it! You have landed a job at that prestigious university as an assistant professor. Although you loved working with K–12, this is your opportunity to make an even greater impact. The biggest challenge—to publish ... or as they say in academia, "PUBLISH or PERISH."

You sent your first manuscript off six weeks ago and today you "have mail." As you look at that line in your inbox, you are anxious to click to open it. Hopefully, this will prove to be your academic "baptism." Your heart is in your throat. You click.

"Dear Mr. Ames, we regret to inform you that your work was not accepted through our blind peer-review process. Thank you for considering Glorious Press at this time. The reviewer's comments are attached."

You hesitate to open the attachment. You think, "not even a 'if you fix x, y, and z' you can resubmit for consideration?"

You open the attachment.

Reviewer One states, "What world are you living in? This is the most unrealistic viewpoint ever. Get a life." At this point you don't even want to see what Reviewer Two had to say.

You slump down in your chair. I was pretty good at being a principal, you think.

What action will you take next?

_____

_____

_____

Suggested Reading

Green and Leonard, *Leadership Intelligence: Navigating to Your True North*, p. 61.

Additional Selected Reading

Palanski, M., K. Cullen, W. Gentry, and C. Nichols. Virtuous Leadership: Exploring the Effects of Leader Courage and Behavioral Integrity on Leader Performance and Image. *Journal of Business Ethics* (August 2014). DOI 10.1007/s10551-014-2317-2.

6

AUTHORS' OPTIONS FOR ABILITY TO INSPIRE SJTS

GET RID OF THE LEADERSHIP CLASS

A. Remind the entire group that this is a leadership program and as such, leadership must be taught.
B. Laugh out loud and respond to the group as if this were a joke. Suggest other ideas.
C. Ask the new professor to "hold that thought." Stop the meeting at this point for a lunch break. Invite the new professor to have lunch with you.
D. Ignore the remark and ask for other options.
E. Other option: _____
_____
_____

FRATERNITY DAYS

A. Ask the department head to address the issue with the students.
B. Tell the Head Resident Assistant to call a meeting and address the issue.
C. Send out a memo to all residents of the dorm stating that all such activities are to be ended immediately under penalty of disciplinary action.
D. Promptly call a meeting of the residents of the dormitory involved and tell them that anyone found involved in such activity will be subject to disciplinary action up to and including expulsion.

CHAPTER 6

    E. Other option: _____

_____

_____

NOT MY JOB

    A. The other members should ask the instructor to step in and intervene.
    B. The other members should step in and support their colleague just as they would in a work setting.
    C. The other members should ask the sick member to drop out of the group.
    D. The other members should accept, without whining, that they will have a lower grade as parts of the project will not be completed; after all, this person is a part of *their* team.
    E. Other option: _____

_____

_____

A ROSE BY ANY OTHER NAME

    A. "I am sure that Dr. Ambrose had a well-thought-out system for handling matters, but I have heard all of those comments I care to hear. Dr. Ambrose is not here, I am."
    B. "I am sure that Dr. Ambrose had a well-thought-out system of handling matters but I prefer a different approach and I would appreciate your best efforts to make the new approach work."
    C. "I am sure that Dr. Ambrose had a well-thought-out system for handling matters, but Dr. Ambrose is not the director now."
    D. "I am sure that Dr. Ambrose had a well-thought-out system for handling matters and I appreciate his heritage, but new approaches can be taken."
    E. Other option: _____

_____

_____

DEFINE "NASTY"

A. Ask the professor how any definition of "nasty" could be acceptable.
B. Define it for the professor and then ask him to explain his actions.
C. Ask the professor what he means by his comment.
D. Tell the professor you will assume by his question that he was, in fact, nasty to the GA.
E. Other option: _____
   _____
   _____

PUBLISH OR PERISH

A. Acknowledge that perhaps you were just not cut out to be an *academic*.
B. Acknowledge that the reviewer is a person just like you are; perhaps they are just wrong.
C. Ask a colleague to read the review and give you their assessment or interpretation.
D. While you are "crying in your beer," search the Internet for local administrative positions.
E. Other option: _____
   _____
   _____

7

LESSONS ON VISION

In *Leadership Intelligence: Navigating to Your True North*, the authors share that "Vision as defined in the LSI model is the end result of a process whereby a leader develops objectives or goals and sets a direction for an organization based on the shared input of all stakeholders. Defining vision is simple. Creating a shared vision and, more significantly, effectively communicating that shared vision, and transforming it into action is the challenge."[1]

The scenarios in this chapter are, in one way or another, related to a leader's vision. If your LSI assessment scores indicate this as an area for needed growth, you should work through the scenarios with a couple of things in mind. First, take particular note of the "Authors' Options" section, which provides responses to each problem at the end of each chapter of SJTs.

In working through the scenarios and reviewing the "Authors' Options," one of two things will happen. You will find disparity between your responses and those of the authors, or you might, indeed, find that your responses coincide with the authors' (see appendix B for a graphic representation). Next, reflect on the information you gained from the LSI assessment. If you acknowledge that vision is an area for growth based on the assessment, ask yourself if this was based on your self-assessment, the circle assessment, or both.

If either or both assessments (self or circle) indicate that you have room for improvement in the area of leader vision *and* you are also finding disparity between your responses and the authors' options, chances are you will find growth by working through these exercises and the accompanying readings. However, be reminded, this will not happen overnight. Growing your leadership intelligence is a worthy endeavor but is a painstakingly time-consuming undertaking. It requires the rewiring of learning patterns

CHAPTER 7

that are ingrained in your most innate thought processes and this takes time. (See appendix B for a graphic representation.)

On the other hand, if you find your solutions and the solutions offered in the "Authors' Options" coincide to a great degree yet your "self" score is lower than the mean for the group shown at the end of your LSI assessment for vision, one of two things is happening. Either you are lacking in self-confidence yet your decision making is solid or, conversely, perhaps you are somewhat overconfident but nonetheless making good decisions.

If the first is the case, working through the scenarios should enhance your self-confidence. The second option (overconfidence) is the one to be most wary of. Leaders in this category many times find themselves derailed as leaders, even though they generally are good decision makers. Working through the scenarios should help to instill the idea that there is more than one acceptable solution to most problems and issues and thus lessen one potential major consequence of overconfidence—the feeling that you have the only viable solution.

If you opt to have a circle or 360-assessment done and find that your solutions and the solutions offered in the "Authors' Options" coincide for the most part and yet your circle scores are outside the standard deviation (available from the LSI team when a circle or 360-assessment is done) LSI for vision, it is possible that a different set of problems is occurring. Perhaps you are selecting the course of action you believe is best for the scenario but, in reality, you would not implement it, or perhaps the problem is one of *perception*. It is much more likely that it is the former, but in rare instances, perception can be the cause of low scores in vision. This could be a case of projection; for example, you may not "look" credible. You will recall from the chapter on credibility in *Leadership Intelligence: Navigating to your True North* that mention was made of how "what you wear" infers or projects an image. Such could be the case in this instance.

Finally, improving your leadership intelligence and "adaptive capacity," as stated in the preface, is a process. As you will recall, the notion of leadership intelligence is predicated on the theory that there is a genetic predisposition toward leadership.

As Marquis and Tilcsik[2] so aptly noted, imprinting may take place during brief sensitive periods of high susceptibility during the formative process, during the teachable moment, or at yet another time of susceptibility, and that, once established, imprints are persistent.

The lessons in this book are to be utilized to grow LSI in this third way—over the long, repetitive process. To that end and to truly be imprinted with any of the competencies, actions for building the various skill sets may be found in appendix C.

"Vision opens the door to opportunities for success for the credible, competent, inspirational leader."[3]

A VISION

Your appointment as Director of Student Life came in late August and by November, three months in, you are seeking a Coordinator of Student Activities. The departure of the former student activities coordinator was under the best of circumstances; she finished her appointment at your sister university in town and her fiancé had proposed.

She did a good job, but with the knowledge of the pending vacancy, a number of students have shared their thoughts regarding the new hire. They have interest in both the programs that are offered, how the programs are managed, and the characteristics and expectations of the new coordinator.

What do you say to the students to create a shared vision for the student activities program?

_____
_____
_____
_____
_____
_____
_____
_____

Suggested Reading

Green and Leonard, *Leadership Intelligence: Navigating to Your True North*, p. 70.

Additional Selected Reading

Dougherty, J. To Get a Commitment, Make a Commitment. *Harvard Business Review: Leadership* (December 2012). Retrieved from https://hbr.org/2012/12/to-get-a-commitment-make-a-com.

CHAPTER 7

LITTLE WHITE LIES

Promotion time is right around the corner and you are somewhat anxious as a new position you would like has come open. Although you have met all the required metrics, you still are not confident you will be selected for the position. You are keenly aware of the politics involved regarding these decisions. Yours is not the only name "in the hopper" for this job and the other candidate has been here longer. However, some questionable history does follow the other candidate.

You are in the boss's office one day and the discussion ensues regarding the potential opening. The boss infers (but does not stipulate) that you will be supported for the position. You leave feeling quite pleased. Time passes for the position to be filled. The other candidate is selected. Although disappointed, you are not completely surprised. That is, you are not surprised until you find out that your boss did NOT support you for the position. You wonder why the boss did not just tell you prior to the announcement.

What do you do?

_____
_____
_____
_____
_____
_____
_____

Suggested Reading

Green and Leonard, *Leadership Intelligence: Navigating to Your True North*, p. 72.

Additional Selected Reading

Bryman, A. Effective Leadership in Higher Education: A Literature Review. *Studies in Higher Education* 32(6): 693–710.

A BUMPY ROAD TO SUCCESS

The head of the Department of Student Services has informed you confidentially that your current position as Director of Student Life is to be eliminated in a cost savings move when your current contract ends. Moreover, she said that she will be handling Student Life services with the support of the coordinators and the department secretary. She has asked you not to mention the forthcoming changes until an official announcement is made in a few days. You honor that request but are anxious about speaking to the members of your department as soon thereafter as possible.

In the interim, of course, rumors begin to circulate about upcoming budget cuts and you are getting questions from your staff about the impact of those cuts on their department. Those questions go politely unanswered as you respond only that you have heard the rumors too.

Simultaneously, rumors begin to abound that further changes are coming to help rectify the funding issues of the college. The announcement about the cuts is made and you call a meeting of your staff.

What do you say?

_____

_____

_____

_____

_____

_____

_____

Suggested Reading

Green and Leonard, *Leadership Intelligence: Navigating to Your True North*, p. 75.

Additional Selected Reading

Gavett, G. What Does Professionalism Look Like? *Harvard Business Review: Organizational Culture* (March 2014). Retrieved from https://hbr.org/2014/03/what-does-professionalism-look-like.

CHAPTER 7

DEMANDING TO DEFEND

You have accepted a position at a new institution as department chair and associate professor. One of your new duties includes chairing dissertations in the newly created doctoral program. You have a handful of candidates, one who is the superintendent of a small, local school district. He is very driven, passionate about his work, and goal-oriented.

About two semesters into the program, he sends you the first draft of his dissertation proposal. After reviewing the first few pages, you realize that he will need a great deal of assistance. Rather than working your way through the remainder of the document, you set an appointment to discuss potential pitfalls and areas that need work.

The two of you meet and have a lengthy discussion regarding modifications that need to be made. The superintendent, although polite, seems taken aback that you are not completely pleased with his work. You explain that this sort of writing—technical, academic writing for a dissertation—is very different in nature from most of the writing he has done prior to this work. He nods in agreement, says he understands, and vows to get the revised document back to you in a timely manner.

A couple of weeks pass and there it is. The new document is an attachment to a brief email. The superintendent thanks you for your prior meeting and assures you that the attached document is now in correct form. You open the attachment as you sigh in relief. You are doing your best to create positive relationships with all the area districts and were feeling a bit uncomfortable about the potential with this district prior to the email.

You open the paper and work through the first ten pages or so. Your heart sinks. This version is not appreciably better than the first. You question your judgment. You question your ability to convey to the superintendent what it is that needs to be done. As you are pondering the best way to move forward, a trusted colleague enters your office.

You discuss the issue with the colleague and she agrees to give the paper a look. After reviewing your concerns, she agrees that you are right on track. You determine that perhaps your input might be better served in writing. You go through the first pages again, this time utilizing the "Track Changes" function in Word. In the email, you explain that perhaps the university writing center might be of value as well.

Four hours later you receive a heated email from the superintendent questioning your judgment and authority. He is insistent that the work he has submitted is excellent and has been evaluated by a subordinate at his work. He tells you that he has intentions of graduating no later than next semester and furthermore is shocked by your stonewalling. He insinuates that you are trying to keep him and his district from improving by denying his timely graduation.

How do you respond?

_____

_____

_____

_____

_____

_____

_____

Suggested Reading

Green and Leonard, *Leadership Intelligence: Navigating to Your True North*, p. 80.

Additional Selected Reading

Witz, G. Are You Decisive? *Leadership Excellence Essentials* (October 2014): 11–13.

CHAPTER 7

SPRING IS IN THE AIR

You have recently hired a new Student Activities Coordinator who is off to a great start. Her work ethic is superior and she finds ways to manage difficult situations with aplomb. She also excels at keeping you informed of events and circumstances related to her work as needed. So, when she calls and asks if you have time to see her, saying that she has something pressing that she needs to discuss, you tell her to come as soon as she can and you will make time to see her.

Seated in your office she tells you that a graduate student enrolled at the college has asked her out. She likes him and wants to know whether going out with him is allowable.

What do you say to her?

_____

_____

_____

_____

_____

_____

_____

Suggested Reading

Green and Leonard, *Leadership Intelligence: Navigating to Your True North*, p. 83.

Additional Selected Reading

Coll, J. Rethinking Leadership Development in Higher Education. *The EvoLLLution: Operations and Efficiency* (January 2016). Retrieved from https://evolllution.com/managing-institution/operations_efficiency/rethinking-leadership-development-in-higher-education/.

ON THE ROAD AGAIN

You enter your office after a 1:00 meeting and are greeted by your unusually agitated secretary who is staring out the huge window directly across from her desk. She begins to explain to you that she has been observing one of her coworkers circling the parking lot for the last 45 minutes waiting for a parking space close to the building to become available.

You are fairly new to the position and are not certain yet of all of the office politics. However, you are aware that the "driver" (also one of your employees) has built a reputation of doing as little as possible at work.

How do you handle the situation?

_____

_____

_____

_____

_____

_____

_____

Suggested Reading

Green and Leonard, *Leadership Intelligence: Navigating to Your True North*, p. 85.

Additional Selected Reading

Gigliotti, R. A., and B. D. Ruben. Preparing Higher Education Leaders: A Conceptual, Strategic, and Operational Approach. *Journal of Leadership Education* 16(1): 96–114.

8

AUTHORS' OPTIONS FOR VISION SJTS

A VISION

A. "Let's form a committee, sit down together, and come to a consensus. I would like to understand what you would like the program to be and what type of director you would like to see hired. Based on that consensus, we can prepare a recommendation to the president about the program and also develop a list of attributes we would like to see in the new coordinator. Together we can create a better program."

B. "Let's form a committee, sit down together, and discuss your ideas and concerns. Based on our discussion, I can prepare a recommendation to the president about the program and then develop a list of attributes that I would like to see in the new coordinator. A better program can be created."

C. "Let's form a committee, sit down together, and I will share with you what we can do programmatically. I can then prepare a recommendation to the president about potential changes to the program. The new coordinator we hire can carry out the approved changes. In that way we can have a better program overall."

D. "Let's form a committee and sit down together to look at what realistically can be done. There are financial limitations that impact both the program and the hiring of a new coordinator. By working together within those parameters, we can have a better program."

E. Other option: _____

_____

_____

CHAPTER 8

LITTLE WHITE LIES

A. Go to your boss and ask him why he did not support you for the position as he inferred he would.
B. Go to your boss and ask him why he did not just tell you prior to the filling of the position if he would not be able to support you.
C. Go to your boss and tell him you are very upset that he lied to you about the position.
D. Go to your boss and ask him why you were not selected for the position. Be prepared for whatever response you receive.
E. Other option: _____
_____
_____

A BUMPY ROAD TO SUCCESS

A. "Yes, it is true that I will be leaving the college. The cuts are unfortunate but necessary. I have enjoyed working with each of you and wish you well."
B. "Yes, it is true that I will be leaving the college. The cuts are unfortunate but necessary. However, no further cuts to this department are planned at the current time. Your work here is essential to the success of the college. Dr. Washington will be taking over the Student Life functions and she will let you know of any further changes."
C. "Yes, it is true that I will be leaving the college. The cuts are unfortunate but necessary. Dr. Washington will be supervising the Student Life function from this point forward and you know that she is fair and experienced. And the new programs being considered should help to move the institution toward a more positive future financially and overall. The future of the college and your futures here seem secure."
D. "Yes, it is true that I will be leaving the college. The cuts are unfortunate but necessary. I wish you well and am optimistic about the future of the college."
E. Other option: _____
_____
_____

DEMANDING TO DEFEND

A. Explain in writing your understanding of the superintendent's desire to finish in a timely manner while holding your position that he is not ready.

B. Ask your colleague to contact the superintendent affirming your position.
C. Resign as chair of the committee and let someone else take a shot at working with this hothead.
D. Allow the superintendent to defend his proposal and fail.
E. Other option: _____

_____

_____

SPRING IS IN THE AIR

A. "You are both adults. If you want to go out with him, go ahead."
B. "You are both adults, but remember that you are a college employee and he is a student. While there is no policy, romantic relationships between students and teachers, or college employees in general, are frowned upon."
C. "You are both adults, but the college has a policy prohibiting relationships between students and faculty or staff. There must be a clear separation between you and the students you supervise or work with as coordinator. If you choose to accept his invitation, you will be in violation of that policy and I would expect your resignation."
D. "Why would you ask me this? You are an adult and must decide for yourself."
E. Other option: _____

_____

_____

ON THE ROAD AGAIN

A. Tell the secretary you appreciate the information, but that she should keep her focus on *her* own job.
B. Tell the secretary you appreciate the information and remind her that this issue is disturbing her work as much or more than her coworker's.
C. Tell the secretary you appreciate the information and call the driver in, asking her what might be the cause of her driving rather than working.
D. Tell the secretary you appreciate the information, call the driver in, and inform her as a warning that you are putting a note in her file of the incident.
E. Other option: _____

_____

_____

9

LESSONS ON EMOTIONAL INTELLIGENCE/ SOFT SKILLS

Being emotionally intelligent means a lot of things. It includes the ability to recognize emotions in ourselves, controlling or regulating those emotions, acknowledging the same in others, and having a social and relationship awareness. Specifically, these last two categories of emotional intelligence—relationship management and social awareness—fall into what is currently commonly referred to as "soft skills." Additionally, with the incredible influx of technology into our lives, many of us are not nearly as "in tune" with others as in the past.

It is *critical*, now more than ever in our rapidly advancing, fast-paced society, that we give top priority to this crucial relationship-building and sustaining skill. With regard to emotional intelligence and the soft skills therein, we must ask—does the leader say what they mean and support that with their actions? The answer to that question defines the soft skills of the leader.

The scenarios in this chapter are, in one way or another, related to a leader's emotional intelligence/soft skills. If your LSI assessment scores indicate this as an area for needed growth, you should work through the scenarios with a couple of things in mind. First, take particular note of the "Authors' Options" section, which provides responses to each problem at the end of each chapter of SJTs.

In working through the scenarios and reviewing the "Authors' Options," one of two things will happen. You will find disparity between your responses and those of the authors, or you might, indeed, find that your responses coincide with the authors' (see appendix B for a graphic representation). Next, reflect on the information you gained from the LSI assessment. If you acknowledge that emotional intelligence/soft skills is an area for growth based on the assessment, ask yourself if this was based on your self-assessment, the circle assessment, or both.

CHAPTER 9

If either or both assessments (self or circle) indicate that you have room for improvement in the area of leader emotional intelligence/soft skills *and* you are also finding disparity between your responses and the authors' options, chances are you will find growth by working through these exercises and the accompanying readings. However, be reminded, this will not happen overnight. Growing your leadership intelligence is a worthy endeavor but is a painstakingly time-consuming undertaking. It requires the rewiring of learning patterns that are ingrained in your most innate thought processes and this takes time. (See appendix B for a graphic representation.)

On the other hand, if you find your solutions and the solutions offered in the "Authors' Options" coincide to a great degree yet your "self" score is lower than the mean for the group shown at the end of your LSI assessment for emotional intelligence/soft skills, one of two things is happening. Either you are lacking in self-confidence yet your decision making is solid or, conversely, perhaps you are somewhat overconfident but nonetheless making good decisions.

If the first is the case, working through the scenarios should enhance your self-confidence. The second option (overconfidence) is the one to be most wary of. Leaders in this category many times find themselves derailed as leaders, even though they generally are good decision makers. Working through the scenarios should help to instill the idea that there is more than one acceptable solution to most problems and issues and thus lessen one potential major consequence of overconfidence—the feeling that you have the only viable solution.

If you opt to have a circle or 360-assessment done and find that your solutions and the solutions offered in the "Authors' Options" coincide for the most part and yet your circle scores are outside the standard deviation (available from the LSI team when a circle or 360-assessment is done) LSI for emotional intelligence/soft skills, it is possible that a different set of problems is occurring. Perhaps you are selecting the course of action you believe is best for the scenario but, in reality, you would not implement it, or perhaps the problem is one of *perception*. It is much more likely that it is the former, but in rare instances, perception can be the cause of low scores in emotional intelligence/soft skills. This could be a case of projection; for example, you may not "look" credible. You will recall from the chapter on credibility in *Leadership Intelligence: Navigating to Your True North* that mention was made of how "what you wear" infers or projects an image. Such could be the case in this instance.

Finally, improving your leadership intelligence and "adaptive capacity," as stated in the preface, is a process. As you will recall, the notion of leadership intelligence is predicated on the theory that there is a genetic predisposition toward leadership.

As Marquis and Tilcsik[1] so aptly noted, imprinting may take place during brief sensitive periods of high susceptibility during the formative process, during the teachable moment, or at yet another time of susceptibility, and that, once established, imprints are persistent.

LESSONS ON EMOTIONAL INTELLIGENCE/SOFT SKILLS

The lessons in this book are to be utilized to grow LSI in this third way—over the long, repetitive process. To that end and to truly be imprinted with any of the competencies, actions for building the various skill sets may be found in appendix C.

"The leader who, through developing his/her leadership intelligence, can also master the ability to recognize and react appropriately to both the rational and emotional sides of an individual has a decided advantage over the leader who lacks those abilities."[2]

CHAPTER 9

COMPASSION

Your new boss (the department chair) appears to be incompetent. Furthermore, she is trying to make your life miserable. Having served as the assistant to the president who is now retired, you have had many years to watch the "up-and-comings" work their charms. And you don't blame them. In fact, you admire their passion and desire to make a difference.

Regardless, as a member of the "ranks" now finishing up your career, you know your place. You do your best to "stay under the radar" and be as helpful as possible. Recently, you turned in paperwork to do a presentation at a conference. The paperwork was returned grossly underfunded. Last week, you asked your new boss about volunteering to fill a service position for the department. The boss tells you that she has someone else in mind for that role.

Today, you are checking your email and you see something from the department secretary. The boss's mother has passed away and the boss will be out for the remainder of the week.

What will you do in regard to the boss's loss?

_____

_____

_____

_____

_____

_____

_____

_____

Suggested Reading

Green and Leonard, *Leadership Intelligence: Navigating to Your True North*, p. 90.

Additional Selected Reading

McClellan, R., D. Christman, and A. Fairbanks. Ulysses' Return: Resilient Male Leaders Still at the Helm. *Journal of Research on Leadership Education* 3(1) (May 2008).

A STITCH IN TIME

She is late again and you are irritated. She is not just a few minutes late: at times she is a half-hour late. It started early in her tenure as a Head Resident Assistant for her dorm and it has not gotten any better despite the admonitions and warnings of the Coordinator of Housing. Now the coordinator is asking for your help as director. When the scheduled meeting ends, you ask the Head Resident Assistant to stay for a brief chat.

She looks like she knows what may be coming—another reprimand or worse—and begins to apologize about being late again as soon as the others have left. You listen intently but hear nothing but the usual excuses that, in fact, are just that—excuses. There seems to be no rational basis for her tardiness.

You start to speak and she interrupts politely saying, "I need to share one more thing with you."

"What is it?" you ask.

She tells you in a quivering voice as tears start to run down her cheeks, "I have been diagnosed with adult attention deficit/hyperactivity disorder (AD/HD) and have been put on medication to treat it."

How do you respond to her?

_____

_____

_____

_____

_____

_____

_____

Suggested Reading

Green and Leonard, *Leadership Intelligence: Navigating to Your True North*, p. 94.

Additional Selected Reading

Rocca-DelGaizo, K., A. B. Frymier, and T. P. Mottet. The Application of Basic Communication Skills to Higher Education Administration. *Journal of the Association for Communication Administration* 32(2) (2013): 87–94.

CHAPTER 9

FUN AT WORK?

Happiness is a highly individualized and internalized feeling, both personally and professionally. While, for purposes of discussion, personal and professional happiness can be separated, the two often carry over and impact each other. Still, being happy in our personal lives does not guarantee happiness in our professional lives nor does the opposite apply.

Beyond whatever carryover exists, a leader has minimal opportunities to impact the personal happiness of organizational members. Conversely, there are things a leader can do to increase potential professional happiness.

Rate each item below on a scale of 1 to 10 (with 1 indicating the lowest importance and 10 the highest) in relation to the item's importance in promoting organizational members' professional happiness. A scoring rubric is provided in the "Authors' Options" section.

A	Encourage organizational members to offer praise when accomplishments are achieved	1	2	3	4	5	6	7	8	9	10
B	Provide access to high-quality training and professional growth opportunities	1	2	3	4	5	6	7	8	9	10
C	At appropriate times, encourage staff members to take earned time off	1	2	3	4	5	6	7	8	9	10
D	Display energy and enthusiasm in working with organizational members	1	2	3	4	5	6	7	8	9	10
E	Ensure that pay and benefits are competitive, fair, equal for equal work, and maximized	1	2	3	4	5	6	7	8	9	10
F	Be cordial and friendly	1	2	3	4	5	6	7	8	9	10
G	Provide organizational members opportunities for decision making discretion (Porath et al., 2012)	1	2	3	4	5	6	7	8	9	10
H	Offer to mentor aspiring leaders	1	2	3	4	5	6	7	8	9	10
I	Provide feedback about performance (Porath et al., 2012)	1	2	3	4	5	6	7	8	9	10
J	Have and share an optimistic outlook as a leader	1	2	3	4	5	6	7	8	9	10
K	Provide equal access to opportunities for promotion	1	2	3	4	5	6	7	8	9	10
L	Deflect praise for successes to the responsible organizational members	1	2	3	4	5	6	7	8	9	10

BACKGROUND

Professional satisfaction and happiness have been shown to be related to worker performance. Therefore, incorporating those behaviors into a leader's repertoire of behaviors enhances the probability of worker satisfaction and happiness as well as organizational productivity.

Green, W. S. M., and E. E. Leonard. The importance of happiness in the workplace. (2012) *Wiley Online Library: Leader to Leader 2012*(63): 62–63. DOI 10.1002/ltl.20012.

Kerns, C. D. Putting Performance and Happiness Together in the Workplace. *Graziado Business Review* 11(1) (2008). Retrieved from http://gbr.pepperdine.edu/2010/08/putting-performance-and-happiness-together-in-the-workplace/.

Porath, C., G. Spreitzer, C. Gibson, and F. G. Garnett. Thriving at Work: Toward Its Measurement, Construct Validation, and Theoretical Refinement. *Journal of Organizational Behavior* 33(2) (May 2011): 250–75. DOI 10.1002/job.756.

Suggested Reading

Green and Leonard, *Leadership Intelligence: Navigating to Your True North*, p. 99.

Additional Selected Reading

McKee, A. Empathy Is Key to a Great Meeting. *Harvard Business Review: Meetings* (March 2015). Retrieved from https://hbr.org/2015/03/empathy-is-key-to-a-great-meeting.

CHAPTER 9

MA'AM, WOULD YOU STEP OUT OF THE CAR, PLEASE?

Your institution's impending accreditation visit looms on the horizon. As Director of Accreditation, tomorrow morning you will pick up the team and drive them back to your institution for the day. The host hotel is downtown and your campus is less than fifteen minutes away.

The morning of the first day of the visit, you arrive at the host hotel fifteen minutes early to greet and gather the group. You walk the visitors to your car, which is parked outside on the curb. Anxious, yet doing your best to stay focused and friendly, you accidently turn the wrong way down a one-way street. You have made it less than a block when you realize your error; you quickly dart down an adjacent street, but alas, there are blue lights in the rearview mirror.

As you pull to the curb, you offer apologies to your guests and prepare yourself for the inevitable. The officer walks up to your window and asks to see your driver's license, registration, and insurance card. You ask your front-seat passenger to excuse you while you rummage through the glove box of the car. Sweat dripping off your brow, you cannot seem to locate your insurance card. You pass the license and the registration to the officer and empty the contents of the glove box into your lap. Your visitors sit quietly... uncomfortably quietly.

As you are fumbling through the papers in your lap, the officer who had earlier retreated to his car returns. He asks you to step out of the car. You turn and look at your passengers, all of whom have stupefied looks on their faces, each of them strangers in a strange town. *You are horrified.* You assure them you will have this all cleared up in a second. You are keenly aware not only how shocking this whole incident is, but also that the clock is ticking on an already absolutely jam-packed day.

You get out of the car. The officer asks you to step around to the back of the vehicle. This is not looking good and you need to get these visitors on to campus.

What do you do?

_____

_____

_____

_____

Suggested Reading

Green and Leonard, *Leadership Intelligence: Navigating to Your True North*, p. 102.

Additional Selected Reading

Hughes, L. W. Leader Levity: The Effects of a Leader's Humor Delivery on Followers' Positive Emotions and Creative Performance. *Journal of Behavioral and Applied Management* 10(3) (2009): 415–42.

SELF-KNOWLEDGE

Warren Bennis (2004), well-known author and leadership expert, says of leaders, "The ruling quality of leaders, adaptive capacity, is what allows true leaders to make the nimble decisions that bring success. Adaptive capacity is also what allows some people to transcend the setbacks and losses that come with age and to reinvent themselves again and again."[3]

Bennis's notion of adaptive capacity can be viewed as an applied amalgamation of the personality traits espoused in the five-factor model of personality. McCrae and John (1992) in describing the five-factor model held that there are "five basic dimensions: Extraversion, Agreeableness, Conscientiousness, Neuroticism, and Openness to Experience."[4] Neuroticism, in this instance, can be further defined as emotional stability.

1. Read each item carefully.
2. Select the answer that best describes how often you engage in the behavior described (A) Always; (B) Often; (C) Occasionally; (D) Seldom; or (E) Never.
3. Circle the letter (A B C D E) of the answer you select.

A scoring rubric is provided in the "Authors' Options" section.

Item	Description	Always	Often	Occasionally	Seldom	Never
A	I like to join multiple groups/organizations	A	B	C	D	E
B	I consider myself imaginative in my approach to tasks	A	B	C	D	E
C	I am even-tempered	A	B	C	D	E
D	I am hard working	A	B	C	D	E
E	I am generally good-natured	A	B	C	D	E
F	I am comfortable personally and professionally	A	B	C	D	E
G	I have a strong sense of curiosity	A	B	C	D	E
H	I am punctual	A	B	C	D	E
I	I tend to be forgiving of mistakes	A	B	C	D	E
J	I remain calm in most situations	A	B	C	D	E

(continued)

Item	Description	Always	Often	Occasionally	Seldom	Never
K	I am active physically and mentally	A	B	C	D	E
L	I seek new approaches	A	B	C	D	E
M	I am trusting of others	A	B	C	D	E
N	I am highly verbal	A	B	C	D	E
O	I am well-organized	A	B	C	D	E

BACKGROUND

The five-factor model of personality has been shown to be related to a variety factors that contribute to leadership success such as job satisfaction (Judge, Heller, & Mount, 2002), life satisfaction (DeNeve & Cooper, 1998), organization citizenship (Chiaburu et al., 2011), and work environment (Ruth, 2016). Aspects of the model, specifically extraversion and agreeableness, have been shown to be positively related to transformational leadership (Judge & Bono, 2000).

Chiaburu, D. S., I. Oh, C. M. Berry, N. Li, and R. G. Gardner. The Five-Factor Model of Personality Traits and Organizational Citizenship Behaviors: A Meta-Analysis. *Journal of Applied Psychology* 96(6) (2011): 1140–66. DOI 10.1037/a0024004.

DeNeve, K. M., and H. Cooper. The Happy Personality: A Meta-Analysis of 137 Personality Traits and Subjective Well-Being. *Psychological Bulletin* 124(2) (1998): 197.

Judge, T. A., and J. E. Bono. Five-Factor Model of Personality and Transformational Leadership. *Journal of Applied Psychology* 85(5) (2000): 751–765. DOI 10.1037/0021-9010.85.5.751.

Judge, T. A., D. Heller, and M. K. Mount. Five-Factor Model of Personality and Job Satisfaction: A Meta-Analysis. *Journal of Applied Psychology* 87(3) (June 2002): 530–541. DOI 10.1037/0021-9010.87.3.530.

Ruth, J. A. (2016). An Examination of the Impact of the Big Five Personality Traits and Work Environment on the Leadership Behaviors of Millennial Generation Employees. *Dissertation Abstracts International Section A* 76 (2016).

Suggested Reading

Green and Leonard, *Leadership Intelligence: Navigating to Your True North*, p. 104.

Additional Selected Reading

O'Neil, D. P. Predicting Leader Effectiveness: Personality Traits and Character Strengths. *Dissertation Abstracts International* 68 (2007): 4178.

LESSONS ON EMOTIONAL INTELLIGENCE/SOFT SKILLS

FEET OF CLAY

As department chair, sometimes you must make decisions that do not make all parties involved ecstatic. As such, you have been directed by the provost to create a new policy regarding the display of overtly political images and the like in faculty offices and spaces. You know this will come with some backlash from tenured faculty. Nonetheless, you move forward in creating a document that you believe will both appease the boss and be palatable to "the troops."

One particularly opinionated full professor, Dr. Green, is not happy that there *is even* such a mandate. Without consideration of how you might handle the situation, she pounds out an email to fellow professors. Doing so, she neglects to notice she has included you in the "group" email. At one point in her tirade, she refers to you as "our boss with the feet of clay." When you receive the email, you are offended and mad.

You hit the "reply all" button and say:

_____

_____

_____

_____

_____

_____

_____

Suggested Reading

Green and Leonard, *Leadership Intelligence: Navigating to Your True North*, p. 108.

Additional Selected Reading

Bawany S. Cover Article: What Makes a Great Leader? *Leadership Excellence Essentials* 32(12) (December 2015): 5.

CHAPTER 9

ROOMMATE ISSUES

Your duties as Director of Student Life call for you to deal with student disciplinary matters and to deal with other problems that arise between students such as arguments or disagreements leading to requests for change of roommates or dormitory residence. The young woman sitting in front of you has made such a request. You call for the Housing Coordinator to sit in on the conference with you.

You ask the young woman her name and what dorm she lives in. She says, "I'm Lily Guess and I live in Stuart Hall."

You ask, "Well, Lily, what is the problem?"

She quickly replies, "I cannot stand to stay one more night in the room with that girl. And I am not going to. I have spent the last two nights in a motel to avoid going back but my parents saw the credit card charge and wanted to know what's up."

She goes on before you can reply. "We fight all the time and do not get along at all. It is so bad it has started to affect my class work. Personally, I think she needs help. Above all, the thing that disturbs me the most is that she is a cutter."

This is a term you are familiar with and it is disturbing.

You say, "I am sorry you have had a bad experience with your current roommate but we may be able to help."

Turning to the Housing Coordinator you ask, "Do we have any rooms available?"

The coordinator replies, "As it happens, a room has become available. But it is a private room."

Jumping at the opportunity, Lily says, "I'll take it."

With the coordinator nodding in agreement, you tell Lily, "We can allow you to move there for the rest of the semester at no additional charge. But, if you elect to stay there next semester you will have to pay the private room price."

Lily is well satisfied with this, thanks both of you, and leaves to begin moving to her new room.

Before the roommate arrives, the Housing Coordinator tells you that she is not surprised. Lily's roommate has not been able to get along with any of her former roommates and she is in her junior year. You ask the coordinator if she has heard about the girl being a "cutter" and she says no.

When the roommate arrives, you tell her that Lily has requested a change and that the change has been granted. Knowing her past history, you begin to talk to her about the issues she has had with Lily and other roommates. She is defensive and says she was the one who should have requested to move. But when you ask her about Lily's allegation that she is a cutter, she becomes silent and begins crying, tears rolling down her cheeks, and finally with a great sighing sob she says, "Yes, I do it to relieve tension."

What should your response be? What should you say?

Suggested Reading

Green and Leonard, *Leadership Intelligence: Navigating to Your True North*, p. 109.

Additional Selected Reading

Tjan, A. K. Flexibility and Persistence: Getting the Balance Right. *Harvard Business Review: Entrepreneurship* (November 2009): 2–5.

CHAPTER 9

DISAPPOINTMENT

The position of dean of the division is coming open on the satellite campus where you work. It is one for which you are well-qualified and in which you are very interested. You have been the chair of your department now for ten years and are ready for a new challenge. You have the respect and admiration of most of the faculty in the division. You recently had a meeting with the vice president of the satellite and he has asked you if you would be willing to serve the institution in that capacity.

The VP has also informed you that an external search for your current position is not in the budget. In preparation for your new position as dean, you discuss possible replacements for your current chair position with the retiring dean. A few possibilities are discussed. After much dialogue, you both settle on one possibility. The dean suggests you speak with this person to determine if there is interest. You do and there is. Both of you are excited about the possibilities.

As the time gets closer to make the transition, you are informed that the circumstances have changed and that the position of dean of the satellite is being repurposed. You will not be getting the job.

What do you do?

_____
_____
_____
_____
_____
_____
_____

Suggested Reading

Green and Leonard, *Leadership Intelligence: Navigating to Your True North*, p. 113.

Additional Selected Reading

McKee, A. Empathy Is Key to a Great Meeting. *Harvard Business Review: Meetings* (March 2015): 2–4.

AUTHORS' OPTIONS FOR EMOTIONAL INTELLIGENCE/SOFT SKILLS SJTS

COMPASSION

- A. Do what you always do. Pick up a sympathy card (but skip the gift card for a meal), sign it, and put it in her box.
- B. Sign the departmental sympathy card and donate $5 toward flowers.
- C. Do what you always do. Pick up a gift card that will pay for a meal, along with a sympathy card, and put it in her box.
- D. Pretend like you haven't heard and do nothing. She certainly hasn't done anything to be kind to you.
- E. Other option: _____
  _____
  _____

A STITCH IN TIME

- A. "With some of the things you have been dealing with like the tardiness, you have taken the right first step. But a diagnosis is not a cure and medication is only effective in helping with your condition. You still have to take responsibility for your actions and find ways to overcome the effects of your condition. Your job hangs in the balance."

B. "With some of the things you have been dealing with like the tardiness, you have taken the right first step. But you still have to take responsibility for your actions and find ways to overcome the effects of your condition."

C. "With some of the things you have been dealing with like the tardiness, you have taken the right first step by seeking out what is causing the difficulties you have been experiencing. And the medication should help. Nonetheless, your position calls for you to be on time to work and to be available at designated times to discharge the responsibilities that are associated with your job. Having taken that first important step, I suggest that you take the next step. There is an excellent counselor on staff who works with individuals with AD/HD. I suggest that you make an appointment with him. He can suggest some strategies to help you with your AD/HD-related issues, starting with being on time. Your lateness must be addressed."

D. "With some of the things you have been dealing with like the tardiness, you have taken the right first step. But your condition is no excuse for consistently being late for meetings. You are still responsible for your actions. If you cannot correct this, you will be dismissed as Head Resident."

E. Other option: _____

_____

_____

FUN AT WORK?

Complete the chart in the "Fun at Work?" section of chapter 9. Then, insert your answers in the "Emotional Intelligence" section of the "Authors' Solutions."

MA'AM, WOULD YOU STEP OUT OF THE CAR, PLEASE?

A. Explain to the officer that you have out-of-town guests in the car on university business. Ask him if you may take a moment to call someone to pick them up as you are waiting.

B. Prior to exiting the car, find the number of the office in your phone and give it to one of the guests to call and ask someone on campus to come and give them a ride as you may be detained for a bit.

C. As you are getting out of the car, make a call to the office for assistance.

D. When you get to the back of the vehicle, let the tears flow. Beg for mercy from the officer and tell him your job is on the line.

E. Other option: _____

_____

_____

SELF-KNOWLEDGE

Complete the chart in the "Self-Knowledge" section of chapter 9. Then, insert your answers in the "Emotional Intelligence" section of the "Authors' Solutions."

*Scale items based on the "Examples of Adjectives, Q-Sort Items, and Questionnaire Scales Defining the Five Factors" (McRae & John, 1992, 178–179).

FEET OF CLAY

A. Hit "reply all" and type: "Dr. Green, To err is human; to forgive, divine. Have a great weekend."
B. Respond only to Dr. Green: "I am troubled by your remarks. Please come see me at your first opportunity."
C. Respond to the group by reminding them that email is a public mode of communication and, as such, nothing should be posted that they would not want to be read in court.
D. There is no need to say anything. Take the high road.
E. Other option: _____

_____

_____

ROOMMATE ISSUES

A. "I know that school is stressful and arguing with roommates only adds to the stress. With that said, I do not know what to tell you about cutting except that it is a bad habit and you must stop." Then end the conference.
B. "I know that school is stressful and arguing with roommates only adds to the stress. I am sorry that you have lost so many roommates." Then end the conference.
C. "I know that school is stressful and arguing with roommates only adds to the stress. And I am sorry that you have lost so many roommates but maybe your

behaviors have something to do with it, especially the cutting. You should seek help."
D. "I know that school is stressful and arguing with roommates only adds to the stress. And I am sorry that you have lost so many roommates. But have you ever thought that your behavior and especially the cutting may be why they choose to leave? I think that a counselor might be able to help. The college has an excellent counselor on call. May I make an appointment with her for you?"
E. Other option: _____

_____

_____

DISAPPOINTMENT

A. Resign your current position and look for another job; the administration lied to you.
B. Call the potential new chair in to inform him of the changes, including that you will not be leaving your current position.
C. File a grievance with the university.
D. Resign your current position as chair so the new person can advance toward his dream; you had mentally moved on anyway. Continue in a faculty job there until you can find a suitable new position.
E. Other option: _____

_____

_____

AUTHORS' SOLUTIONS FOR SJTS

Disclaimer: On the following pages are the authors' recommended solutions, rationale, and reasoning for rejection of alternative solutions. These recommendations are in no way intended to supersede work policy or act as legal advice to the learner. These are actual situations encountered by the authors including the solutions they enacted at the time and place of the circumstance.

CREDIBILITY SOLUTIONS

MEDICALLY INCOMPETENT

Best Response: *B. Explain to his boss that based on your interactions you do not believe he is competent to continue; however, you would appreciate consideration for keeping him onboard as long as is feasible for the organization.*

Rationale: Being as kind as is possible in his last days is the most humane thing to do. Keep the bigger picture in perspective without losing sight of this most important thing.

Rationale for rejecting the alternate responses:

- A. Your friend, as noted above, is not himself. He probably will NOT recognize your attempt to be helpful or compassionate but will potentially see your remarks as threatening and possibly undermining.
- C. Although an acceptable choice, as a friend, if you do no more than this, more than likely down the road you may feel responsible for actions out of your control that others may take. Speak up while you have the opportunity.
- D. Although an understandable response, it may anger and frustrate his boss, ultimately leading to problems for you (in the immediate future, such as not being allowed to help your friend, or in the long term). Be honest and forthcoming.

SMALL THINGS MATTER

Best Response: *C. Take and pay for the coffee as the professor ahead of you paid.*

Rationale: While his gesture is nice, accepting free items (even a cup of coffee) when everyone else pays is not appropriate.

Rationale for rejecting the alternate responses:

- A. His offer may be well-intended but others are paying.
- B. Tipping may be appropriate but only if you pay.
- D. Not a good idea.

EXCEPTION TO THE RULE

Best Response: *B. Meet with the faculty member and discuss the possibility of another option.*

Rationale: Since you do not have the authority to take matters into your own hands, doing so (as suggested in option A) could come with repercussions; therefore, rationally discussing the issue is the more desirable option.

Rationale for rejecting the alternate responses:

- A. As stated above, taking matters into your own hands could cause repercussions; remember, not everyone thinks the same way you do.
- C. Although this is an acceptable option, it does not suggest a very high level of emotional intelligence; strong leaders demonstrate this trait.
- D. "Passing the buck" to your dean further negates your authority and may suggest to the dean that you are neither capable nor needed.

A HELPING HAND

Best Response: *A. "Being new here, I would really like to get a feel for the activities the students are involved with. We both have very full schedules. It would help both of us if you would allow me to attend some of the activities in your place. But if you are not comfortable with that, I understand. What do you think?"*

Rationale: This response addresses the issue fully by addressing the subordinate's comfort and asking their opinion.

Rationale for rejecting the alternate responses:

- B. This response is too directive.
- C. This response is headed in the right direction but stops short of addressing the subordinate's feelings.
- D. This response places the burden on the subordinate.

FAILURE TO LAUNCH

Best Response: *B. Remind Phil that a pass at the department level is just the beginning. Recommend to Phil that he withdraw his materials prior to your writing a letter of nonsupport.*

Rationale: You could just let Phil make his own decision after you write your letter, but giving him the option to withdraw prior to submitting your letter is more humane and kind.

Rationale for rejecting the alternate responses:

A. You should not write a letter of support, just because the department did, if you disagree.
C. This is a strong response as well, however, once you have put your thoughts in writing as chair of the department (and those thoughts indicate your lack of support), they are a matter of record and remain in his personnel folder.
D. If you feel he will not be successful at the college level, you do not have to tell him so; however, to suggest to him that it might go otherwise would not be forthright and would be disingenuous. It also does not convey your understanding of policy and procedures, which could very well undermine your relationship or position with Phil in the future.

A BOND IS FORMED

Best Response: *A: Allow the interviews to proceed without comment.*

Rationale: To build trust, you must extend trust. Having taken the step to delegate this authority to the coordinator, you must allow him the latitude to perform the task unfettered, barring the sharing of any negatives that have become known to you. Once again, consistency and ensuring that your actions match your words have a powerful effect.

Rationale for rejecting the alternate responses:

B. This action is contrary to the process you put in place that you would only disclose negatives. Showing preferences (indicating those you feel are best-suited) moves toward substituting your judgment for that of the coordinator.
C. The same rationale as for item B applies here. Moreover, if one candidate is singled out, the director may interpret this as your choice, forgo interviews, and realize that your word and actions do not coincide.
D. Unless some other caveat or circumstance has arisen, this delay is unnecessary. It might send the wrong message to the coordinator.
E. This option speaks to the quality of the candidates indirectly. It is better to let the coordinator form his own opinion and base his judgment on that opinion.

COMPETENCE SOLUTIONS

HOW MUCH IS ENOUGH?

Best Response: *B. Based on your review, the dossier clearly is insufficient; make an appointment with Dr. Smith to discuss your analysis of the materials and offer her a chance to withdraw them rather than forcing you to deny her promotion.*

Rationale: The current precedent should change immediately; however, the humane thing to do is to allow Dr. Smith to withdraw her materials rather than have a documented rejection at the dean level.

Rationale for rejecting the alternate responses:

A. You will have sent both Dr. Smith and all the others the message that this sort of work is acceptable; you should not promote someone who has not earned the promotion.
B. This is an acceptable action; however, it lacks compassion for Dr. Smith who will be caught completely by surprise when she gets the news.
C. As the old adage goes, "it's too late to shut the barn gate after the horses are all out." Making a reverse turn would appear to be placing blame, which generally never solves a problem. Move forward based on the current situation.

LEADERSHIP ORIENTATION

Best Response: There is no best response as the scored responses denote the individual's emphasis of a given orientation as a higher education leader: Model the Way; Inspire a Shared Vision; Challenge the Process; Enable Others to Act; or Encourage the Heart.

Enter your rating from the "Authors' Options" for "Leadership Orientation" in the "Lesson on Competence" section. Then insert your answers in the appropriate space below:

Scoring:

Model the Way = sum items 1, 7, and 14

___ + ___ + ___ = _____
 1   7   14   Models the Way total score

Inspire a Shared Vision = sum items 4, 8, and 11

___ + ___ + ___ = _____
 4   8   11   Inspire a Shared Vision total score

Challenge the Process = sum items 3, 6, and 15

___ + ___ + ___ = _____
 3   6   15   Challenge the Process total score

Enable Others to Act = sum items 2, 10, and 13

___ + ___ + ___ = _____
 2   10   13   Enable Others to Act total score

Encourage the Heart = sum items 5, 9, and 12

___ + ___ + ___ = _____
 5   9   12   Encourage the Heart total score

Categories based on the work of Simon Black.[1]

Interpretation: The scores represent your emphasis on a given orientation as a higher education leader. The higher the score, the more prominent that orientation emphasis is likely to be in your leadership activities.

YOU'RE NOT THE BOSS OF ME

Best Response: *D. Carry on as if the remark had not been made.*

Rationale: Sometimes you just have to rise above the fray. They are going to do what they are going to do; exhibit class and move on.

Rationale for rejecting the alternate responses:

A. The only time to be an autocrat in the current era is when there is a fire in the building.
B. Basically, this would be another unwise autocratic response.
C. Looking for a short tenure as the new chair? Trying to invoke fear is a great way to make that happen.

SEE AND BE SEEN

Best Response: *B. Set a schedule leading up to and following chapel that will have you visiting all of your assigned areas of responsibility.*

Rationale: Perception is often reality. It is important to fulfill your responsibilities from day one.

Rationale for rejecting the alternate responses:

A. If you are unsure, this might be a viable option; otherwise, going back to her may seem to indicate that you lack initiative.
C. Even though chapel is an important activity and deserves attention, leaving other responsibilities unattended is not appropriate.
D. The time will come when delegation is needed. This is not the time.

YELLING

Best Response: *A. Invite your assistant chair in for a visit first thing in the morning. Inquire about the incident and the yelling. Admonish your assistant chair in a professional manner and ask her to apologize to the coordinator.*

Rationale: Yelling is never an acceptable behavior . . . unless there is an active shooter in the building. Even if the coordinator has done something to offend the assistant chair, it is not acceptable for her to yell at her.

Rationale for rejecting the alternate responses:

B. This is a good response, but does not clear the air between your employees.
C. Unless your assistant chair has a history of yelling, this response would be an excessive one on your part.
D. Just because you are close friends with the assistant chair, do not assume the coordinator was at fault. Setting the scenario up as described in option D can complicate things to an even more difficult level.

IF *IS* BROKEN, FIX IT

Best Response: *C. Secure permission and appoint student managers to oversee the student workers and charge the managers with the responsibility of reporting broken equipment and checking IDs.*

Rationale: With only student workers, no one else is responsible for on-site supervision. Student managers can be held accountable.

Rationale for rejecting the alternate responses:

- A. Monitoring is ineffective if no further action is taken. With the same workers and no direct supervision, the problem is unlikely to be resolved.
- B. See the rationale for item A. It applies equally here.
- D. Checking up the ladder may become necessary, but it is best to take the initiative, make the decision, and solve the problems as they arise within your purview.

ERASING 100 "ATTA-BOYS"

Best Response: *A. Rather than internalizing the one negative evaluation, the leader should take the feedback as an opportunity to improve in a particular area.*

Rationale: When you ask for feedback, expect that some of it will be less than stellar. Knowing this up front should help you be open to helpful criticism. Growing your competence and "perception" of competence is the goal.

Rationale for rejecting the alternate responses:

- B. We all have room for improvement. All of us . . . always. Ignoring negative feedback is downright dangerous.
- C. Certainly, as a leader, you cannot wear your feelings on your sleeve; read it, reflect on it, grow from it, and get over it.
- D. You might hope the offending evaluator will leave but, in fact, if you are doing your job (making tough decisions), you will *always* have "naysayers." As "they" say—"it just goes with the territory."

ABILITY TO INSPIRE SOLUTIONS

GET RID OF THE LEADERSHIP CLASS

Best Response: *C. Ask the new professor to "hold that thought." Stop the meeting at this point for a lunch break. Invite the new professor to have lunch with you.*

Rationale: As mentioned earlier in the scenario, this new faculty member is not highly regarded by others; perhaps you have just been afforded a clue as to why. Based on the remark, apparently the new faculty member does not have an appreciation for what is at the core of your business. This is a good opportunity for the two of you to interact and for you to mentor him as well.

Rationale for rejecting the alternate responses:

A. This is not a remark that you want to make; your expectation is that everyone else obviously does know.
B. If you overtly ignore the remark, the new faculty member may either feel ridiculed or he may assume his position was correct since it was not rejected.
D. Same as B.

FRATERNITY DAYS

Best Response: *D. Promptly call a meeting of the residents of the dormitory involved and tell them that anyone found involved in such activity will be subject to disciplinary action up to and including expulsion.*

Rationale: Some issues require a firm and unbending stance. Harassment and bullying fall into this category.

Rationale for rejecting the alternate responses:

A. This falls under your purview and should be handled accordingly. Of course, you will want to alert the department head as to your course of action.
B. Delegation is not appropriate in this instance. Firm action is required by an authority figure.
C. A memo is a weak alternative to a face-to-face meeting.

NOT MY JOB

Best Response: *B. The other members should step in and support their colleague just as they would in a work setting.*

Rationale: As a leader, one must recognize the inequalities in all of life. It may not be fair to have to pick up an extra bit of load, but it is the humane thing to do. Great leaders rise above the minutiae.

Rationale for rejection of other responses:

A. The scenario is clear about the illness of one of the members. The group should resolve this without interference from the professor.
C. The ill student has enough on their plate at the moment.
D. Failure is not an option; everyone should pitch in and make the project a success.

A ROSE BY ANY OTHER NAME

Best Response: *B: "I am sure that Dr. Ambrose had a well-thought-out system for handling matters, but I prefer a different approach and I would appreciate your best efforts to make the new approach work."*

Rationale: As leaders, we learn many things from many people but the one most important lesson we learn is to be ourselves. We cannot be our predecessors nor will those who succeed us act as we would. Be yourself and be firm but polite about the direction you think the organization should go.

Rationale for rejecting the alternate responses:

A. While tempting, this response is a little too empathic.
C. The same rationale as for option A applies here.

D. This response is temping and might actually be a starting point but stops short of asking for cooperation.

DEFINE "NASTY"

Best Response: *A. Ask the professor how any definition of "nasty" could be acceptable.*

Rationale: Be careful that there are those out there who will try to excuse their actions by utilizing camouflage. Don't get sucked in. You cannot win. If this strategy is yielded, you can bet the professor is, in fact, guilty. Stay on point by turning the question around on him. Then explain your expectations for future interaction with the graduate assistant.

Rationale for rejecting the alternate responses:

B. If you define it for him, then he will seek an alternative definition, which by his standard does not make him in the wrong.
C. Like option B, he will make the definition suit his behavior.
D. This is a good solution but, again, it is setting the conversation up for debate. You have given him his due process by asking him if he acted inappropriately. His desire to avoid the question should be ignored.

PUBLISH OR PERISH

Best Response: *B. Acknowledge that the reviewer is a person just like you are; perhaps they are just wrong.*

Rationale: It is important, especially in a new role, to remain optimistic. It is easy in unfamiliar territory to feel uncomfortable, particularly when you are faced with failure. Then, more than ever, it is key to focus on positives and options that "might be" rather than "buying-in" to failure.

Rationale for rejecting the alternate responses:

A. Do not assume the worst over one review.
C. This is a good option as well, but option B allows for internalization and reflection.
D. Same as A.

VISION SOLUTIONS

A VISION

Best Response: A. "Let's form a committee, sit down together, and come to a consensus. I would like to understand what you would like the program to be and what type of director you would like to see hired. Based on that consensus, we can prepare a recommendation to the president about the program and also develop a list of attributes we would like to see in the new coordinator. Together we can create a better program."

Rationale: The emphasis in this narrative is "we." A shared vision requires the inclusive "we."

Rationale for rejecting the alternate responses:

- B. The narrative here is "I"-centered, which is not conducive to creating a shared vision.
- C. Same as option B.
- D. While setting parameters should occur at some point, it is not the best starting point.

LITTLE WHITE LIES

Best Response: D. Go to your boss and ask him why you were not selected for the position. Be prepared for whatever response you receive.

Rationale: Since your boss told you (or inferred) earlier that he would support you, then one of two things has happened—either your boss lied to you or the decision was out of your boss's hands. If it is the first case, then don't expect your boss to suddenly be forthcoming; if it is the second case, then you have asked a fair question and you may get to the reason you were passed over.

Rationale for rejecting the alternate responses:

A. See rationale above.
B. This is a good option except if your boss lied to you; regardless of ALL circumstances, this is still your boss. Act accordingly.
C. Same rationale.

A BUMPY ROAD TO SUCCESS

Best Response: C. *"Yes, it is true that I will be leaving the college. The cuts are unfortunate but necessary. Dr. Washington will be supervising the Student Life function from this point forward and you know that she is fair and experienced. And the new programs being considered should help to move the institution toward a more positive future financially and overall. The future of the college and your futures here seem secure."*

Rationale: This response deals fully with the upcoming changes but gives positive assurances for the future both individually and organizationally.

Rationale for rejecting the alternate responses:

A. This response is going in the right direction but stops short of expressing concern for the future.
B. This response deals with the organizational issues but not personal issues of concern.
D. This response, once again, is going in the right direction but stops short.

DEMANDING TO DEFEND

Best Response: *A. Explain in writing your understanding of the superintendent's desire to finish in a timely manner while holding to your position that he is not ready.*

Rationale: The fact that you are concerned about creating good public relations with the local school districts becomes even more critical as you do the right thing in this situation. Always be as fair as you can be, while standing by your principles.

Rationale for rejecting the alternate responses:

B. Although your colleague concurs with your assessment, if you drag him into the situation, he may be reluctant to help you in the future; furthermore, the superintendent may see this as the two of you ganging up on him.
C. This certainly is an option but interferes with your larger vision of creating good relations with area districts. The situation may yet be rectifiable.
D. Same as C.

SPRING IS IN THE AIR

Best Response: C. *"You are both adults, but the college has a policy prohibiting relationships between students and faculty or staff. There must be a clear separation between you and the students you supervise or work with as coordinator. If you choose to accept his invitation, you will be in violation of that policy and I would expect your resignation."*

Rationale: You have a professional obligation to the college and to the coordinator to be frank about the ramifications of her question.

Rationale for rejecting the alternate responses:

A. This response fails to discharge your professional responsibility to your subordinate.
B. This response approaches fulfilling your professional responsibility but stops short and leaves open the question of consequences.
D. This response not only fails to discharge your professional responsibility to your subordinate but is also argumentative.

ON THE ROAD AGAIN

Best Response: C. *Tell the secretary you appreciate the information and call the driver in, asking her what might be the cause of her driving rather than working.*

Rationale: Ignoring this sort of behavior demoralizes those trying to do their jobs properly.

VISION SOLUTIONS

Rationale for rejecting the alternate responses:

A. It is possible (probably unlikely, however) that there is a good explanation for the driving. Also, you already have some limited knowledge that the driver is not a good employee.
B. Although you would probably be correct in this assumption, it does nothing to deal with the slacker.
D. Always give a verbal warning before putting concerns in writing.

EMOTIONAL INTELLIGENCE/SOFT SKILLS SOLUTIONS

COMPASSION

Best Response: *C. Do what you always do. Pick up a gift card that will pay for a meal, along with a sympathy card, and put it in her box.*

Rationale: The Golden Rule is a good application here. "Do unto others as you would have them do unto you." She may not deserve your kindness, but she certainly needs it.

Rationale for rejecting the alternate responses:

A. Although tempting, remember, anyone can be kind to a friend.
B. This is an acceptable response as well; however, think on this—don't let the behavior of others dictate your own behavior.
D. Now you are really abasing yourself—take the high road.

A STITCH IN TIME

Best Response: *C. "With some of the things you have been dealing with like the tardiness, you have taken the right first step by seeking out what is causing the difficulties you have been experiencing. And the medication should help. Nonetheless, your position calls for you to be on time to work and to be available at designated times to discharge the responsibilities that are associated with your job. Having taken that first important step, I suggest that you take the next step. There is an excellent counselor on staff who works with individuals with AD/HD. I suggest that you make an appointment with him. He can suggest some strategies to help you with your AD/HD-related issues, starting with being on time. Your lateness must be addressed.*

Rationale: This is a serious diagnosis at any age and is recognized as a handicapping condition. In this response you have shown empathy for her situation, recognized officially her condition, and offered assistance. You have also made it clear it is up to her to follow through and seek further assistance with her one major issue.

Rationale for rejecting the alternate responses:

A. This response begins well but fails to address the entire problem.
B. Same as A.
D. Same as A.

FUN AT WORK?

Best Response: There is no best response as the scored responses denote the individual's orientation toward leadership: egocentric, people-oriented, or task-oriented.

Scoring:
Insert the appropriate scores in the scoring system below:

Egocentric = sum items D, F, H, and J

___ + ___ + ___ + ___ = ___
D   F   H   J   Egocentric total score

People-oriented = sum items A, C, E, and L

___ + ___ + ___ + ___ = ___
A   C   E   L   People-oriented total score

Task-oriented = sum items B, G, I, and K

___ + ___ + ___ + ___ = ___
B   G   I   K   Task-oriented total score

Interpretation: The scores represent your tendencies toward behaviors that promote organizational member professional happiness. The higher the score, the more prominent this orientation is likely to be in your leadership activities. Maximum score for each category is 40.

MA'AM, WOULD YOU STEP OUT OF THE CAR, PLEASE?

Best Response: *A. Explain to the officer that you have out-of-town guests in the car on university business. Ask if you may take a moment to call someone to pick them up as you are waiting.*

Rationale: When your emotions are running high (as they could be in this situation), try to call on your logical brain for help. Take yourself out of the situation and ask yourself what your most trusted adviser or mentor might do in this situation.

Rationale for rejecting the alternate responses:

B. The person might be unavailable or the person's voicemail may respond. You are showing your visitors your lack of ability to respond appropriately to stress by choosing this option. You have left the resolution to mere chance.
C. A good solution, if you get lucky and can attend to the call quickly; however, if the officer wants to speak with you, he or she might not appreciate your making your phone more important than the issue at hand.
D. Tempting, but don't allow this or anything similar to happen. Remind yourself that this is a temporary situation and that you need to behave rationally. Call on your rational brain!

SELF-KNOWLEDGE

Best Response: There is no best response as the scored responses denote the individual's personality tendencies as related to the five-factor model of personality: extraversion, agreeableness, conscientiousness, neuroticism (emotional stability), and openness to experience.

Scoring:
For the letter selected for each item, give yourself the following points. Then total the scores for each category.
A = 5; B = 4; C = 3; D = 2; E = 1

								Total
1.	Extraversion	1	+	11	+	14	=	(___)
2.	Agreeableness	5	+	9	+	13	=	(___)
3.	Conscientiousness	4	+	8	+	15	=	(___)
4.	Neuroticism (emotional stability)	3	+	6	+	10	=	(___)
5.	Openness to experience	2	+	7	+	12	=	(___)

Interpretation:
The wide acceptance of the five-factor model and the extensive research indicating the relationship of the model's factors to leadership and life success make it essential that

leaders understand their personality tendencies and dispositions. The results of this scale indicate your self-perception in relation to the aspects five-factor model. A higher score in a given area indicates that your personality tends to reflect characteristics of that factor.

FEET OF CLAY

Best Response: *D. There is no need to say anything. Take the high road.*

Rationale: It is easy to be offended; it is difficult to ignore an offense. Ignore the offense and allow others to consider the source. You have other "fish to fry."

Rationale for rejecting the alternate responses:

A. Although a response like this would allow the offender to realize they have copied you (as well as the entire department), it basically only stops the complaining at an obvious level. People who complain will do it by the water cooler, on the phone, etc.; the point is, you CANNOT stop it, you can just divert it. When you do this, you have just put yourself on the same level with the assailant.

B. Reminding this employee that you are the boss is a waste of time—more than likely, someone this foolish will not listen to your message in person either. You should, however, make a "note" to the file in the event there are additional issues.

C. A remark like this would be considered "preaching to the choir." Again, you are putting yourself on a level with the offender—don't go there.

ROOMMATE ISSUES

Best Response: *D. "I know that school is stressful and arguing with roommates only adds to the stress. And I am sorry that you have lost so many roommates. But have you ever thought that your behavior and especially the cutting may be why they choose to leave? I think that a counselor might be able to help. The college has an excellent counselor on call. May I make an appointment with her for you?"*

Rationale: By responding in this fashion, you have shown empathy for her situation and have provided reassurance and assistance. Anything further borders on interfering with her outside the college and your professional purview.

Rationale for rejecting the alternate responses:

A. A strictly business response but it lacks empathy and shows little or no concern for her situation.

B. A response of this nature lacks empathy and sends the message that you do not want to be a party to the problem.
C. A more empathetic response but it stops well short of recognizing her human predicament.

DISAPPOINTMENT

Best Response: *D. Resign your current position as chair so the new person can advance toward his dream; you had mentally moved on anyway. Continue in a faculty job at your current institution until you can find a suitable new position.*

Rationale: Even in the unlikely event that the change in plans was to keep you from advancing your career, "you can't fight city hall." Most likely the change in plans was much bigger than one person. Accept that the reason was not personal and move forward.

Rationale for rejecting the alternate responses:

A. A hasty decision is rarely the best one and bitterness only hurts the holder.
B. Staying in your current position is certainly an option; however, having already served in this role for ten years, it is likely that everyone will benefit from someone with new ideas.
C. There are times in your career when filing a grievance may be warranted; unless you have evidence of arbitrary or capricious behaviors on the part of the administration, this is not one of them.

APPENDIX A

Small Group Cards

(Cut out individual letters and laminate for class use)

A	B
C	D
E	F

APPENDIX B

LSI Interpretation Chart

When reviewing your "self" or "circle" graph, keep in mind there can be four outcomes for each of the five skill sets, as well as your total leadership intelligence score. Begin by considering your total LSI; then, move to your category of greatest relative weakness. Remember, a strength overused can become a liability.

APPENDIX B

LSI Self/Circle Assessment Matrix*	
High Self/High Circle *Most Desirable Orientation*	**Low Self/High Circle** *A Problematic Orientation* (Preferred over a High Self/Low Circle orientation)
• *Strong in category and strong self/circle congruence suggests that leadership orientation is well developed and recognized.* • *Skill enhancement is advisable for continued success.*	• *Low self scores and high circle scores indicate a leadership orientation lacking in leader self-confidence.* • *Leader growth is needed although the circle has confidence in the leader.*
High Self/Low Circle *A Problematic Orientation*	**Low Self/Low Circle** *Least Desirable Orientation*
• *Leadership potential for egocentric/narcissistic orientation.* • *Weak circle congruence suggests a need for leader growth and development of the leader-circle relationship.* • *Without growth derailment is likely.*	• *Orientation with most room for growth.* • *Though there may be congruence between the self and circle scores in this orientation, this leadership orientation suggests a need for leader growth and development of the leader-circle relationship focused on success.*

*The self and circle scores, as well as the congruence of the self and circle scores, vary along a spectrum from low to high. For each scenario, the authors' choices are typical of high self/high circle responses. This matrix represents the most likely outcomes and orientations.

APPENDIX C
Activities to Improve Your Leadership Intelligence

Now is a good time to reflect on the navigational analysis from *Leadership Intelligence: Navigating to Your True North*. Let's consider that you are the driver for a chartered bus with thirty-five travelers to a landmark tourist adventure 600 miles away. You have made many trips in your lifetime that were 600 miles or longer, but perhaps you have never been to this particular destination. Maybe some of those on the bus are older than you are and have driven longer. Perhaps, even, some of them have been to the destination at hand on a previous occasion. Prior to embarking on the trip, you have several options in preparation for the trip.

Regardless of how you choose to prepare, each of your travelers has their own expectations regarding the trip. Some may wish you would drive faster, others might wish you would have taken the more leisurely, scenic route. Still others may question the detours, pit stops, and even the announcements you make. All of these factors (and many others) will inform their feedback on your performance as a driver.

After returning from your destination and reflecting on the trip yourself, you too might consider different decisions you could make if you had the chance to "drive the bus again." Your own reflections, as well as the passengers' feedback, will certainly leave an impression—how strong an impression might depend upon the degree of congruence between your perception of the trip and theirs.

In order to improve the next trip (and not to imply that this one was a bad one), the driver needs to be reflective, ask for feedback, and plan for the future. This planning (for improvement) could include a myriad of things from using a more updated map (or GPS) to planning to take the trip at a better time of year. It will include both study and action.

The same planning for improvement, study, and action holds true for leadership intelligence (LSI). The scenarios in the field book are given to help the leader consider a myriad of possible solutions to different problems and to become more effective and efficient at resolving them. Whether considered individually or in a group setting with the rich dialogue, discourse, and reflective dynamics that such may generate, study leading to action will be the best teacher and will provide a clear, direct route to success in increasing your leadership intelligence.

As a leader becomes aware of and chooses the construct or skill set (credibility, competence, inspiration, vision, or emotional intelligence) that he or she would most like to improve, in addition to the exercises in the book, the following activities are recommended. For the best results, these activities should be planned and acted upon over a period of not less than six months.

To improve your credibility, while working through the book scenarios, as odd as it may seem, plan to write an article or research paper for publication to share your experiences and expertise. This is *not* a one-week assignment. You should set aside (at a minimum) weekly time to work on organizing, researching, and writing the article or paper. This will not be just for the sake of obtaining facts and information, it will also be for the purpose of presenting them. How you present yourself in your writing is a huge part of your credibility.

If you rush through and/or are sloppy, you leave a distinctly poor impression with the reader (think emails, memoranda, and even handwritten notes). As a leader, in any written correspondence, if you give the facts and figures without ensuring that they are valid, reliable, and, in fact, real, again you lose credibility. As you are preparing your paper, work to triangulate (using multiple data sources) to ensure your credibility. A second option would be to undertake case study readings about historical or contemporary figures you admire and believe to be credible, and to reflect on what about these individuals makes them credible. These case studies could also be incorporated into your article or research paper.

To improve your competence, while working through the book scenarios, align yourself with a mentor in your field of leadership and meet with them regularly.

Try to find opportunities not only to interact with this person on an informal basis but, more importantly, to "shadow" this person. Write down a list of questions to ask about how he or she arrived at a specific solution or why he or she took a certain position. Take the time to discuss with your mentor other solutions that might have been considered.

Talk to this person about typical problems and issues he or she encounters and how he or she approaches resolving them. Spend as much time talking about the why as the what, the how, and the timing of his or her decisions. Don't be timid when asking about technical matters. Technical matters form the basis—the what—that people are to accomplish.

To improve your ability to inspire others, while working through the book scenarios, join a speakers' bureau. Or, conversely, become a coach, sponsor, or leader for a children's athletic, drama, music, or scout group. You might rather choose to join adult groups such as a neighborhood watch, owners' association, or civic group such as a Rotary or Lions Club where you will have the opportunity to lead by your words and actions.

As a member of a speakers' group, seek opportunities to present motivational or inspirational messages regularly. The same is true if you choose to become a volunteer coach, sponsor, or leader of children's groups. Be sure that you give motivational pitches regularly to the children. With adults, volunteer to lead or to participate in group activities. Being actively involved in the suggested activities should present ample opportunity to both observe and to be a part of inspirational activities and should have a corresponding positive impact on your overall ability in this area.

To improve your vision, while working through the book scenarios, embark on a personal improvement plan. This can be anything from a physical, spiritual, mental, or emotional area of your life. The idea is to choose an area for self-improvement and then to map out a six-month plan to reach a specific goal.

As Covey would say, "begin with the end in mind."[1] Once you have created the plan—and make it very detailed and specific—enact the plan. At the end of each month, evaluate and reflect on your progress and then adjust your plan accordingly. Or, as an alternative strategy, plan an event or series of events for your family or another group with which you are associated. Be sure to engage family or group members in the planning processes to produce a shared vision regarding each event. The personal plan or the planning of events should engage you actively in the give-and-take of reaching a personal decision that impacts your individual plan (or the consensus) that is needed for visionary action.

To improve your emotional intelligence/soft skills, while working through the book scenarios, commit yourself to involvement with a charitable, civic, school, religious, or other worthwhile organization that is not a part of your work. Focus your energies not only on the betterment of the cause or organization, but specifically on the people affiliated with it. Be intentional in your desire to encourage, support, and embolden them. Or, as an alternative strategy, volunteer to assist in projects sponsored by local civic groups that involve working with people in need, or volunteer to work in an appropriate capacity at a hospital or nursing home, or volunteer to assist youth groups in your community. The emotional impact of serving others selflessly should provide opportunities for growth in your emotional intelligence.

The combination of intense review of SJTs along with the activities briefly described above over a period of time will ensure growth in your chosen leadership intelligence skill set. Not only will your skill set scores improve, but more importantly, your leadership capacity will improve. Your road to success as a leader will be like an up-to-date GPS with all the latest features, newest maps, and best route guidance available.

NOTES

PREFACE

1. Warren G. Bennis and Robert J. Thomas, *Geeks and Geezers: How Era, Values, and Defining Moments Shape Leaders* (Boston: Harvard Business School Publishing, 2002).
2. Ibid.
3. Warren G. Bennis, "The Seven Ages of the Leader," *Harvard Business Review* 82(1) (January 2004): 46.
4. Catherine Bond Hill, Welcoming Remarks, Vassar (2010). Retrieved from https://www.vassar.edu/remarks/convocation/2010b/president-hill.html.

INTRODUCTION

1. Wanda Maulding Green and Edward E. Leonard, *Leadership Intelligence: Navigating to Your True North* (Lanham, MD: Rowman & Littlefield, 2016).

SITUATIONAL JUDGMENT TESTS

1. Michael McDaniel and Deborah Whetzel, "Situational Judgement Tests," Lecture, IPMAAC Workshop (June 20, 2005).
2. Michael McDaniel, Frederick Morgeson, Elizabeth Finnigan, Michael Campion, and Eric Braverman, "Use of Situational Judgment Tests to Predict Job Performance: A Clarification of the Literature," *Journal of Applied Psychology* 86(4) (August 2001): 730–740.

NOTES

CHAPTER 1

1. Christopher Marquis and András Tilcsik, "Imprinting: Toward a Multilevel Theory," *The Academy of Management Annals* 7(1) (June 2013): 195–245.

CHAPTER 3

1. Christopher Marquis and András Tilcsik, "Imprinting: Toward a Multilevel Theory," *The Academy of Management Annals* 7(1) (June 2013): 195–245.
2. Simon A. Black, "Qualities of Effective Leadership in Higher Education," *Open Journal of Leadership* 4(2) (2015): 54–66. Retrieved from http://file.scirp.org/Html/2-2330076_57195.htm.

CHAPTER 5

1. Christopher Marquis and András Tilcsik, "Imprinting: Toward a Multilevel Theory," *The Academy of Management Annals* 7(1) (June 2013): 195–245.
2. Wanda Maulding Green and Edward E. Leonard, *Leadership Intelligence: Navigating to Your True North* (Lanham, MD: Rowman & Littlefield, 2016).

CHAPTER 7

1. Wanda Maulding Green and Edward E. Leonard, *Leadership Intelligence: Navigating to Your True North* (Lanham, MD: Rowman & Littlefield, 2016).
2. Christopher Marquis and András Tilcsik, "Imprinting: Toward a Multilevel Theory," *The Academy of Management Annals* 7(1) (June 2013): 195–245.
3. Green and Leonard, *Leadership Intelligence: Navigating to Your True North*.

CHAPTER 9

1. Christopher Marquis and András Tilcsik, "Imprinting: Toward a Multilevel Theory," *The Academy of Management Annals* 7(1) (June 2013): 195–245.
2. Wanda Maulding Green and Edward E. Leonard, *Leadership Intelligence: Navigating to Your True North* (Lanham, MD: Rowman & Littlefield, 2016).
3. Warren G. Bennis, "The Seven Ages of the Leader," *Harvard Business Review* 82(1) (January 2004): 46.
4. Robert R. McCrae and Oliver P. John, "An Introduction to the Five-Factor Model and Its Applications," *Journal of Personality* 60(2) (June 1992): 175–215.

NOTES

COMPETENCE SOLUTIONS

1. Simon A. Black, "Qualities of Effective Leadership in Higher Education," *Open Journal of Leadership* 4(2) (2015): 54–66. Retrieved from http://file.scirp.org/Html/2-2330076_57195.htm.

APPENDIX C

1. Covey, S. R. *The Seven Habits of Highly Effective People: Restoring the Character Ethic* (New York: Simon and Schuster, 1990, c1989).

ABOUT THE AUTHORS

Wanda Maulding Green is an educational leadership faculty member at the University of South Alabama and has served in leadership roles in both K–12 and higher education. She is coauthor of the book *Leadership Intelligence: Navigating to Your True North*.

Edward E. Leonard is a retired school superintendent and higher education administrator. He currently teaches leadership courses at the University of South Alabama and is coauthor of the book *Leadership Intelligence: Navigating to Your True North*.